PUBLIC POLICY STUDIES IN AMERICAN GOVERNMENT

Edgar Litt, General Editor

THE PUBLIC VOCATIONAL UNIVERSITY

Captive Knowledge and Public Power

THE PUBLIC VOCATIONAL UNIVERSITY
Captive Knowledge and Public Power

EDGAR LITT
University of Connecticut

HOLT, RINEHART AND WINSTON, INC.
*New York   Chicago   San Francisco   Atlanta
Dallas   Montreal   Toronto   London   Sydney*

Foreword to the Series

A series devoted to the consequences of American public policy ought, at the outset, to indicate why it came into being. What has been lacking in the scholarly literature is overt analysis of the political consequences of policy on human institutions and on the life style of human beings themselves. A review of the literature convinced the editor, and his colleagues who are to contribute to the series, that the vast analytical skills of political scientists have for too long been directed at the "input" side of politics, the ways in which policy is fashioned or administered out of the mélange of groups competing for public favor. Scholars have studied the behavior of organized interest groups, the calculations of administrative and policy experts, and the meaning of concrete policies for the totality of the political system itself. Yet, in an era where federal policies themselves are major sources of impact and of innovations on society, it is crucial that the scope of our inquiries not be restricted.

The scholar's responsibility extends to an evaluation of policy-forming agencies in terms of clear and realistic values and to an evaluation of the impact of policy "outputs" on the social system. Such responsibility has been asserted by one critical voice in the present epoch in this way:

> Of basic importance is the modern redefinition of "politics." No longer does the term refer to the promotion of justice or the search for the best organization of social life. The term now refers to "who gets what, when, how" or to some similar concept, which focuses not on justice but on power. This focus makes political science more quantifiable and political scientists more pliable and useful for the powers that be. At the same time it severs the study of politics from any direct bearing on the task of developing institutions and organizations in the service of human needs.[1]

The volumes in this series will raise this issue for the distribution of power in the American society, the civil liberties of the individual in times of immense governmental control, the quality of personal and political education received by black and white Americans, and the distribution of housing and other social goods in our urban centers. In our view, this perspective best accounts for the processes and quality of our political life. Moreover, these studies build on the intellectual tradition of public policy exploration that has importantly contributed to the maturation of the field of political science itself.

Storrs, Connecticut   E. L.

---

[1] Christian Bay, "The Cheerful Science of Dismal Politics," in Theodore Roszak (ed.), *The Dissenting Academy* (New York: Pantheon, 1967), p. 3.

Preface

It is now commonplace to assert that American higher education is deeply involved in national politics. Federal support of education, the rash of student protest movements on campuses throughout America, and reactions from conservative politicians and political groups underscore the accuracy of this statement. Yet, in an era where federal policies themselves are major sources of impact and conflict, the scope of political inquiry should not be restricted by these manifestations of education's political import. It is my contention that the American system of higher education is a captive domain. Moreover, the roots of that captivity extend beyond the ambitions of politicians, radical students, and professional scholars. The roots of the new captivity are found in the meshing of universities and the federal government, an interlocking of function and purpose that precedes the conflicts reported in our newspapers.

In addition, the political capture of higher education is located in the maturation of a new knowledge system, one that I call interchangeably the public vocational university or the welfare state university. As the text describes in detail, the public vocational university is most usefully characterized by three functional relationships that set it apart from other colleges and universities in the American experience. First, the public vocational university is highly dependent on federal direction and support; that is, the uses of knowledge are political in nature. Second, the public vocational university is internally rationalized in process and routine in order to fulfill its public mission best. This means that local control by faculty, students, or administrators is weakened in the interest of external compliance with political directives. Third, the process of the public vocational university is essentially in teaching applied, impersonal knowledge. The public vocational university trains passive students in the application of those skills and techniques most needed by the political technostructure that directs it. In essence, the public vocational university trains its students to work for public definitions of higher education and thus to serve the state uncritically. In the process, more humanistic uses of education in personal and political education are weakened.

A year at the University of California in Berkeley provided me with the opportunity to synthesize the thoughts that have gone into this book. I had the invaluable opportunity to reassess basic data about students and educational policies and to discuss these interests with resident scholars, such as Martin Trow and Paul Heist. In addition, I enjoyed the hospitality of the Department of Political Science, in particular the intellectual stimulation and sociability of its chairman, Professor Aaron Wildavsky. I am indebted not only for the rewards of personal and professional friendship, but also for the contributions that this experience have made to the ideas presented in this book.

Herbert J. Addison and his associates at Holt, Rinehart and Winston have made invaluable contributions to the quality and form of this book and its companion volumes in the Public Policy Studies in American Government series. In addition, my fellow scholars and contributers to the Public Policy series, men such as Michael Parenti and James Farganis, have generously provided me the gift of constructive and honest criticism.

Storrs, Connecticut   E. L.
May 1969

Contents

PART II   CURRICULUM, POLITICS, AND STUDENT WELFARE

PART III   HUMAN DEVELOPMENT AND POLITICAL LEARNING

PART I
THE POLITICAL SIGNIFICANCE OF THE PUBLIC VOCATIONAL UNIVERSITY

Introduction

If ed. contribute to imperialism, what should we do?

The relationships between the political and educational institutions of a modern society are complex and involve the fabric of human behavior itself. One way to comprehend the public consequences of formal education is to examine the organization of intellect designed to propel the national interest. The public vocational university—sometimes referred to later as the welfare state university—is such a creation. Designed to develop the uses of applied knowledge and academic training, the public vocational university is able to prosper only in a society whose resources are significantly allocated to produce useful knowledge. Constructed on a broad scale and processing thousands of students, the public vocational university has been able to gain cultural acceptance only because higher education has now been opened to the sons and daughters of parents without a college education. Thus, in the American lower-middle-class culture, with its emphasis on both the practical and innate benefits of higher education, the public vocational university conveys *the* accepted meaning of higher education to unprecedented numbers. The public vocational university is also a product of rapid adaptation in which older university types, such as the pure research graduate school and the humanistic liberal arts college, cannot cope with the scope and size of public expectations about higher education.

Functions performed by an institution are usually unrecognized by those who act in its immediate milieu. Thus, the public vocational university must first be defined in terms of the structural changes that have influenced educational and political realms. Chapter 1 traces the development of the public vocational university from the interlocking relationships between universities and federal bureaucracies that have shaped public knowledge since World War II. The relations between the public vocational university and the political economy that nurtures it for political purposes do not exhaust a structural analysis of the new mainstream in our knowledge-based society. Thus, Chapter 2 examines the internal mechanisms of the university and the selection of personal and educational values it enhances. The public vocational university mediates between the personal qualities shaped by family and peers and the collective civic culture located in the corporate and governmental spheres. One significant theme in the public vocational university's development is the shift from collegiate to national authority problems. A second significant theme is the decline of local autonomy and power on the campus. In addition, the public vocational university is characterized by a curriculum designed to train and socialize masses of students in the ways of the national political order. This shift from education to training and from basic to applied learning is important because it enhances the function of the public vocational university as a tool of the state.

The definition of the public vocational university is not limited by the structural relations between knowledge and power within the society and the specific campus on which vocationalism is dominant or ascending. It is important to inquire into those values and processes that are not maximized in the public vocational university. Chapter 3 examines the personal and political consequences of student culture, curriculum, and faculty relations as guided by public vocationalism. Chapter 3 also examines ways by which a university might be made less a captive of the internal rigidities and public directions that have shaped the public vocational university. The political impact of formal education is found in the ongoing processes of the educational system. The public vocational university, as the applied version of social knowledge's formal rationality, provides the laboratory in which the political expectations of our organized and stratified society are shaped for the next generation.

The public vocational university is not the creation of malevolent or ignorant men. On the contrary, its large size and vast scale are designed to provide educational opportunities for thousands of students. Its formal rules and arrangements are designed to maximize order and process within a complex enterprise. Its emphasis on applied training is a natural result of the belief that citizens must be socialized for the state and the industrial system. Its fear of emotion and independent action are also natural results of disbelief in the viability of any other union of power and knowledge. Criticisms of the public vocational university must be tempered by an understanding of its nature and the forces that have shaped it in the knowledge-based American society.

Chapter 1
Knowledge, Power, and Higher Education

In an agrarian society, trapped in the cycle of poverty and ignorance, both the transmission and acquisition of knowledge depend on the whims of tribal customs and haphazard reports of itinerant visitors. An elite society, which is ruled by a cohesive priesthood or an aristocratic class, carefully guards its knowledge and only selectively extends it to the sons and daughters of the ruling strata. In a populist society characterized by an enormous scope of "grass roots" communication, education and knowledge become personalized at the mass level and are infused with a plebian hostility toward any who claim special intellectual or political competence.

It is only in the postindustrial society that education and polity reach their mutual zenith. In a postindustrial society, a complex mix of democratic procedures and highly centralized organizations, knowledge becomes the core instrument of development and progress, the touchstone to social mobility and national power. Moreover, in the postindustrial society, the instruments of knowledge are in constant tension, the broadest dissemination of skills and ideas is balanced against the restraints of government and the managerial elite. Knowledge becomes both a resource for human liberation and a primary device to ensure social control among agitated masses. The educational systems of military cliques and religious orders seem pale in comparison with the contemporary international communication of skills and ideas. The transmission of traditional wisdom, encompassing the norms of a static society, is archaic amid the specialized centers of learning that propel our modern society. For in no other time or place in recorded history has formal education and its by-products had such an intimate relationship to the life style and opportunities of the ordinary citizen. Knowledge and the agencies of knowledge, ordered in scientific discourse and public institutions, become the master instruments of the creation and distribution of human values.

Once the ornament of a frivolous aristocracy, once infused with a mélange of ethnic and regional interests, higher learning now seems too serious to be entrusted to the pluralist array of student groups, faculty guilds, and boards of regents. In fact, as the relationships between public policy and the instruments of abstract learning become more explicit, the presentation itself of knowledge becomes the critical instrument of power and mastery over men. In such a cultural apparatus is the debate between public issues and private sensibilities increasingly waged.

No resource of modern life—not wealth or numbers or political power itself, resources to which education is intimately related—more vividly determines our aspirations and our public life than higher learning. Let discontent appear among young intellectuals, and plenary conferences are held to cure such latent alienation. Let the demands of new social movements obtain sufficient visibility, and some segment of our educational system will respond by creating programs to eradicate poverty and salvage our core cities. Let war efforts increase and our universities will not only devote increased resources to research, but also serve as forums for debate and action.

THE INTERPLAY OF POLITICS AND HIGHER EDUCATION

An issue becomes political when it is a matter of governmental concern, a subject of extensive debate among concerned citizens.

A series of issues may be considered about the justice of specific decisions, the roles performed by actors in their articulation, and the implications of specific behavior for men and institutions. When, in fact, such events become the normal mode of conduct, they may be justified in the elaboration of myths or ideologies devoted to the "larger" comprehension of specific events.[1]

The relations between educational and political institutions have changed the public significance of the university. It is the thesis of this book that there has developed a public vocational university supported by federal funds, directed by political decisions, and dedicated to the production of applied knowledge useful to the leaders of our political order. This university is becoming dominant in the American educational sector. It is usually large, public, and located in an urban locale. It is typified by Michigan State with its CIA projects and American University with its role in Project Camelot. The public vocational university is a captive of federal governmental support and direction. In fulfilling government needs, the public vocational university shapes the future direction of American higher education to a greater degree than do Amherst or Oberlin with their liberal arts emphasis or than the proud private universities such as Yale and Princeton. Indeed, as all universities increasingly turn to governmental support the distinctions between public and private, research university and teaching college are lessened and higher education becomes dominated by the concepts of public vocationalism in the service of the state.

Until recently, privatism for the collegiate administration was an underlying guideline. Rooted in the domains of founding religious orders or private benefactors, the public implications of American universities were seldom global; indeed, they seldom extended beyond the state's boundaries. Before World War II, the development of most American universities is best studied in terms of the play of local forces:[2] the progressive spirit that fostered the fruition of the political and academic realms in Wisconsin and Minnesota; the Republican business conservatism that led to the formation of Ohio State University; the cultural values that fused the doctrines of Dewey to feminine emancipation at Sarah Lawrence; the separatist dependency that until recently

[1]See Harold D. Lasswell and Abraham Kaplan, *Power and Society* (New Haven, Conn.: Yale University Press, 1950), pp. 116–125.
[2]Allan Nevins, *The State Universities and American Democracy* (Urbana, Ill.: University of Illinois Press, 1964).

made intellectual tombs of Catholic, black, and fundamentalist Protestant colleges. It is this exaggerated localism—exaggerated in importance if not in truth—that animates most political studies of earlier higher education.[3]

However, treating university administrations as so many local governments (and, thus, essentially autonomous and powerful) was congruent with the fragmented political structure of American higher education itself. For it is doubtful if any area of policy and power has had a more diverse institutional base in a nation without a major national university of counterpart to the coordinating French Ministry of Education or English University Grants Committee.

The myth of collegiate privatism (and such historical evidence as gives it substance) stressed the autonomy of the educational institution and its relative powerlessness in external public policy. The power of the burgeoning federal government and the business corporation could not be treated in isolation; but, with rare exception, the university, in concert with local pressure groups, was accorded that splendid autonomy befitting institutions performing services for more powerful agencies of society.

Today, the autonomy and privatism that characterized the university of the past is being shattered. Rather than isolation from a national political context, the role of the student, faculty, and administration is being recreated and readjusted in response to increasingly complex demands upon the educational institution. The strains of institutional mediation today are evident in the words of a former university president operating without the insulation of private, hierarchical control:

> It is interesting that American universities, which pride themselves on their autonomy, should have taken their special character as much or more from the pressures of their environment as from their own inner desires; that institutions which identify themselves either as "private" or as "state" should have found their greatest stimulus in federal initiative; that universities which are part of a highly decentralized and

[3]See, for instance, Malcolm Moos and Francis E. Rourke, *The Campus and the State* (Baltimore: The Johns Hopkins Press, 1959); Thomas H. Elliot, "Toward an Understanding of Public School Politics," *American Political Science Review,* 53 (December 1959), 1032–1051.

varied system of higher education should, nevertheless, have responded with such fidelity and alacrity to national needs; that institutions which had their historical origins in the training of "gentlemen" should have committed themselves so fully to the service of brute technology.[4]

The culture of the university, then, comprises the first element in a political analysis of the higher learning. The political conflicts among faculty and administrators (those faculty and alumni most responsive to the college and those scholars pushing against the home-guard interests in response to national professional interests), the impact of intellectual and "collegiate fun" student subcultures—all are viewed within the new framework of interpenetration, expansion, and federalization, a framework in which the old clarity of the university as an independent social agency is being quickly eroded.

In the older tradition, the diversity of internal forces existed within the more or less autonomous realm of the university. However, in the era of the federal-grant university (itself merely one element in the industrial framework of knowledge production), the institutional milieu is shaped more by developments in national space research than by changes in the complexion of local industry, is affected more by the professional norms of university administrators and their reference groups than by local alliances among the university president and a clique in the metropolis, and is directed more by the flow of federal funds than by the inclinations of private philanthropy.

Similarly, the internal rules and regulations applicable to students becomes democratized and extended, as "student rights" becomes the objective of organizations applying the techniques of boycott, collective bargaining, and informal negotiation.[5] So, too, do the ceremonials of university internal unity and detachment from the external world become more atrophied as devices signifying institutional harmony. As the mass media and fluctuating moods of youth culture cast the semblance of intellectual purpose in adolescent terms, the separation of life from learning that marked the Whig concept of university administration, (namely

[4]Clark Kerr, *The Uses of the University* (Cambridge, Mass.: Harvard University Press, 1963), p. 49.
[5]See Nathan Glazer, "Student Politics in a Democratic Society," *The American Scholar,* 36:2 (1967), 202–217.

one that balanced all interests within the college), becomes more difficult to maintain.

When universities "socialized" farm boys and second-generation immigrants, the problems of self-regulation were less likely to counter the neutral inclinations of efficient university administration. But what the the functionaries in the universities to do as the number of precocious cosmopolites, products of an open and urbane culture, grow in number? After all, institutional privatism was not only an arrangement to sort out intellects and candidates for jobs; it was also an administrative convenience for guiding adolescents through the periods of sexual- and self-awakening. Today, the norms of conventional respectability that provided the basis for the daily performance of an organizational routine must confront the modishness of a modern culture whose youthful "tastemakers" are described in these terms: "They buy their clothes at Paraphernalia and they feel compelled by their peers to have mature opinions on sex and pot and LSD and God knows what else. . . . They have to be in on things that girls at Spence and Chapin don't have to be."[6] So, too, are the institutional arrangements of the university highly dependent on the volatility of mass movements and governmental policies. In the uneasy coexistence that as a quirk of historical accident places mature professionals in proximity to youthful students, these external developments can have dramatic effects on the university. Thus, political concerns about "urban poverty" can bring together a corps of specialists whose impact can quickly change the climate of a placid urban campus. Similarly, young politicians have cultivated national university attention in order to reap quick political capital. For example, in 1967 black civil rights militant Stokely Carmichael gained speedy national attention after appearances at the University of California, Harvard, and Columbia. In turn, Carmichael was able to convert the publicity into subsequent invitations to the campuses of black Southern colleges.

Moreover, the degree of internal collegiate control exerted within the university government becomes more subject to the political consequences of enormous external forces. Attachments to professional disciplines and job mobility among the professoriat combined with the growth of collectivistic social organizations

[6]Richard Snickel, "Privileged Class in a New York Private School," *The New York Times Magazine* (March 12, 1967), Sec. 6:1, pp. 26, 107–122.

among the student youth have now eroded that solidarity of institutional authority that once made the university a bastion of administrative conservatism.[7] The impact is curiously mixed, for if American universities took on the coloration of an anti-intellectual society, the splendid isolation from national political concerns in America did provide some opportunities for institutional innovation. But in the main, these were the solid accomplishments of liberal arts colleges devoted to particular standards of intellectual, communal, or esthetic performance.

The influence of such colleges as Oberlin, Reed, Amherst, and Haverford rested in part upon the absence of high-quality competition in much of the academic marketplace. When institutional restraints blocked out ideas, the cultivation of excellence under the leadership of devoted men gave a handful of liberal arts colleges an impressive position of strength. Under such circumstances, academic student cultures and high status were accompanied by strong, continuing faculty involvement. This institutional pattern, so different from the more "modern" pattern of strong presidential authority and a highly bureaucratic university structure, led to broader participation in university affairs. The institutionalization of educational experimentation, rather than the Whig quest for undefined balance and efficiency, had a binding effect, attaching men of intellectual and cultural distinction to the collegiate orbit. A typical process in the high-quality liberal arts college is described by Clark and Trow:

> The faculty recruited by the charismatic leader, or attracted by the changes he made, takes over after he leaves. Their self-appointed role is to insure the continuity of the college's new character, and their authority takes on this conserving function. Often a faculty council, or some other representative body of the faculty, becomes the key policy-making unit; in other cases authority becomes lodged formally and informally in the hands of department heads and senior department members. In either case, strong faculty control

[7] On the academic man as an itinerant entrepreneur of intellect, see Irving Howe, "Beleagured Professors," *The Atlantic Monthly,* 215 (November 1965), 115–118; for an insightful report on the new student organizational apparatus see *Order and Freedom on the Campus,* a publication of the Western Interstate Commission for Higher Education and the Center for the Study of Higher Education, Berkeley, Calif., 1965.

henceforth plays a role in attracting and binding faculty. . . . In a sense, a faculty that captures control is also captured in return, committed by involvement in policy making; after a half-dozen years, a man has often invested too much of himself to leave. . . . This binding effect of faculty control appears to work in the direction of supporting vigorous academic subcultures in the student body by holding on a campus faculty members with serious intellectual interests who would otherwise have left.[8]

The general excellence of these cultural pacesetters in American higher education is supported historically, yet there is a growing tendency toward reduced institutional influence among the "little elite" of academia.[9] In the face of national trends (and federal resources), the quality of education is endangered in the liberal arts colleges, whose institutional patterns are no longer viable in a world characterized by accelerated change. Institutional conservatism, designed to preserve past innovations, is faced with the growth of specialized institutes. Thus, the university with an established culture and a firm institutional identity must accommodate the accumulated outside pressures of individuals, institutions, and organizations.[10]

It is only by the most concerted efforts that some institutional influence can be maintained. Before the Civil War, a large college had six hundred students; today, central campuses of state universities run to thirty thousand. This has reduced the institution's ability to maintain its own autonomy and strong influence over

[8]Burton R. Clark and Martin Trow, "Determinants of College Student Subcultures," in T. Newcomb and E. Wilson (eds.), *College Peer Groups* (Chicago: Aldine Publishing Company, 1967), p. 41.
[9]The contribution to scholarly productivity of graduates from such small liberal arts colleges as Reed, Swarthmore, Oberlin, and Antioch is documented by C. A. Knapp and F. N. Greenbaum, *The Younger American Scholar: His Collegiate Origins* (Middletown, Conn.: Wesleyan University Press, 1965); on the support of intellectual permissiveness during the McCarthy period, consult Paul F. Lazarsfeld and Wagner Thielens, Jr., *The Academic Mind* (New York: The Free Press, 1958), p. 128.
[10]A former provost at Wesleyan finds that conservatism to innovation becomes a permanent feature of universities organized about some integrating collegiate principle. See Joseph C. Palamountain, "Power Structures in the University," *Antioch Review,* 26:3 (1966), 299–306.

academic and cultural life. Thus, some men (usually university presidents and administrators) note the decline of institutional control and personal authoritarianism in dealing with students and faculty, while other men (usually social critics) emphasize the negative aspects of reduced interpersonal contact. The loss of enforced piety and interpersonal intellectual stimulation, as well as the loss of academic isolation and the ability to provide a counterculture to national vocational uses of knowledge are consequences of the reduced institutional autonomy in the governing of American universities.

THE IMPACT OF POLITICS ON THE UNIVERSITY

The combination of ideas, "adolescent fun," and class routines comprising university life has always produced impatience among educated men. Such critics claim that the old institutions and the courses of study they provide are such that the serious business of national survival and economic growth cannot abide the useless traditions of educational institutions and the cultural pretentions of their faculties. The impatience may reach such proportions in time of national crisis that the established system of higher learning is dismissed out of hand, deemed to be hopelessly unresponsive to the new needs of mass, popular education.[11]

A marginal institution (an agency clearly subordinated to the interests of more powerful sectors of society) may develop the social impetus for change and seek to work important, if incremental, transformations in the distribution of social justice. But an institutional sector that is clearly in the center stage of the national political economy is functionally integrated, despite the protestations of utopians with other models in mind. Elite universities imparted that combination of skill and sensibility appropriate to the sons and daughters of a selective, and fairly small, professional class. Populist universities formed among the states in the aftermath of the land-grant college acts were committed to the cultivation of useful skills and trades critical to a developing

[11]See Robert M. Stamp, "Educational Thought and Practice during the Years of the French Revolution," *History of Education Quarterly,* 6:3 (1966), 35–49.

economy. Universities established by men devoted to sacred symbols sought to accommodate the theological and the academic, to encourage academic exploration within the accommodating framework of an atheistic creed. Of course, universities with each cultural tendency are still visible on the academic landscape.[12]

Yet the central tendencies are more significant, for it is in the unified framework of purpose, culture, and ideology that the political significance of the contemporary knowledge system may be located. Both as a research organization and as a training establishment, the modern university has become intimately involved with the national economy and the state. The exchange of ideas, people, and contracts between university departments and research institutes and their counterparts in private industry and government agencies tends to merge these organizations and to assimilate the life style of their staff. Thus, universities become but one element in the continuous development of a scientific and technological society. The functional reality of the modern educational system is that the important skills for personal and developing large-scale public enterprises become the university's curriculum. In this sense, the collegiate enterprise functions as one gatekeeper to the development and processing of skills useable in organizational form. Today's starkly functional view of intellect is reflected in the relegation to "cultural adornments" of those intellectual concerns once so strongly emphasized in the Western humanistic tradition:

> In engineering and science the number of graduates per 1000 of the population is 9 in USSR and 10 in the USA The different points reached by these two countries in their advance towards the technological society is indicated by the fact that in Russia the percentage of science and engineering graduates to all graduates is 55 whereas in America it is 21. . . . *The extra output of American graduates in the humanities and social sciences mainly reflects the profession-*

---

[12]"The university . . . is of the Church, but it isn't the Church. Yet the connection is strong enough to link Notre Dame—if it wants to remain Catholic —to the fortunes of the Church on the one hand and to the requirements of worldly scholarship and learning on the other" (Peter Schrag, "Notre Dame: Our First Great Catholic University?" *Harper's,* 234 [May 1967], 49).

alization of the tertiary sector of American industry and may be viewed as an adornment of the affluent society, which Russia has yet to become.[13]

The centrality of higher education in the production of skills and talent appropriate to contemporary organizational concerns is a commonplace in popular and academic discourse. The shift from cultivation and transmission of skills to their active creation signifies the impetus of the new technological relationship. In the decade between 1950 and 1960, 796,000 new jobs were created in education; an additional 161,000 positions were created in related social services. More important, however, the educational process itself became more visibly and fully committed to the systematic production and transmission of useful skills based on the ability to manipulate abstract symbols. The social consequences of the scramble for the fruits of organized skills are becoming characteristic of our society. Because only advanced educational institutions can award the credentials of skilled competence, the pressures in the pursuit of excellence and tangible rewards become immense: On the one hand, parents are admonished that "no family with two children should ever attempt the private school route if it is making less than $25,000 a year"; on the other, educators make the observation that "the present scramble to translate achieved educational status into organizational advancement has much in common with the fierce competition of early business capitalists."[14]

In larger context, the direct translation of knowledge into power and status has accentuated the rationalization of intellect and professional life styles. The slow sifting out of talent in a society committed—in theory—to the democratization of educational opportunities begins early in a youngster's life. These changes have only recently affected the sluggish and decentralized base of the American educational system. However, the impetus of functionality has not yet run its course:

[13]H. A. Halsey, "The Changing Functions of Universities in Advanced Industrial Societies," *Harvard Educational Review,* 30 (Spring 1960), 121–22 [emphasis added].
[14]The quotations are respectively from Richard Schnickel, "Privileged Class in a New York Private School," *The New York Times Magazine* (March 12, 1967), Sec. 6:1, 107 and David Bazelon, "The New Class," *Commentary,* 42:2 (1966), 49.

The bureaucratization of the high school is not, of course, merely a peculiar consequence of the search for academic talent in the "cold war" but a manifestation of the general trend toward the rationalization of daily activities in all spheres of contemporary life. With the progressive differentiation and specialization of functions in modern society, we expect an intensification of attempts to maximize the efficiency of identifying and developing the talent within the population. The identification and development of talent is without question a legitimate concern of the high school and there are indications that this concern is beginning to stimulate the organization of talent programs at the junior high and elementary school levels.[15]

The functionally collective purposes of the higher learning in processing skills and knowledge useful in organized form has, of course, numerous ramifications. Perhaps the most critical of these changes is the "bureaucratization of social mobility" that blurs the distinction between a "liberal" and a "vocational" education. One major justification of a university has been that it is designed to provide job training and that this purpose is uppermost in the minds of its students. By contrast, there has often been a dissenting theme, namely that the university is not merely a service station for immediate social demands, but rather a place of critical inquiry, whose fruits are neither imminent nor directly functional to the career goals of its students.

The functional purpose of education blurs this distinction in the way it expands educational opportunities to the less academic and converts intellectual skills into pragmatic vocational channels. The direct vocational pull of education is evident among working-class youth, who often lack family or other models of academic achievement. In expanding college opportunities on the functional model, a major problem has been to convince these youngsters and their parents that college education will "pay off," that the advanced training will be useful on the job market. First, the proximity of the junior or community college increases the prob-

---

[15]Aaron V. Cicourel and John I. Kitsuse, *The Educational Decision-Makers* (Indianapolis: The Bobbs-Merrill Company, Inc., 1963), p. 139. However, the authors find that the distribution of talent is, in fact, based essentially on the organizational processing of test scores in the schools—bureaucratic procedures and coding become prime determinants of discovered talent.

ability of college attendance among those without the heritage of academic culture. Second, demonstrated relationships between colleges and employment mobilize parental support for the collegiate aspirations of their children. One series of studies shows that working-class parents not only supported college for their children, but also, in fact, were more optimistic about their children's success when the job-related advantages of college were emphasized.[16] On the other hand, efforts to enlist parental support on the basis of intrinsic interest in ideas or civic awareness were failures. Thus, as higher education expands, its vocational purposes are more directly emphasized in the curriculum and "college plant." Concomitantly, it is in the areas with the most traditional relations to jobs (such as education, engineering, and business administration) that the bulging lower-status college population appears.

However, the functionalism of education is also significantly, if less obviously, important among more talented students in that an intrinsic interest in ideas—the root of a liberal education—is the mainstay of organizations using innovating proposals and research as a normal part of their business. It is this routinization of intellect and its translation into corporate form that provides the unprecedented power of the emphasis on the functional uses of higher education. Professional norms and values become a major consequence of exposure to higher education. Unlike the period of Corporate Capitalism, individual skill in dealing with abstractions becomes the most important transportable asset, while collective talent is the essential need of all organized activities. The distinction between the "liberal" proclivities of the potential intellectual and the more pragmatic view of the university as skill-providing service station seems, to contemporary educational realists, a romantic indulgence dating to the supremacy of the "free professions" (law, medicine, theology) in higher education.

Sensing the new currents of a society dependent on the de-

---

[16]See "College Image and Student Selection," in *Selection and Educational Differentiation,* report of a conference sponsored by the Field Service Center and the Center for the Study of Higher Education, Berkeley, Calif., 1960; T. R. McConnell, "Differential Selectivity of American Higher Education," in Kenneth E. Anderson (ed.), *The Coming Crisis in the Selection of Students for College Entrance* (Washington, D.C.: National Educational Association, 1960); Marjorie Fullers, "The Junior College: Social Experimentation," *Commonweal,* 193 (October 1966), 9–11.

velopment of new ideas, and articulating an epistomological framework of our folkways, scholars coin new concepts fitting the new functionalism between knowledge and political economy. Humanists dispel the gloom of cultural decline in the new "Ideapolis," fashioned from national need and federal grants. The elements of cultural renewal are not contained in the musty remnants of some classical heritage of Great Books or in public oratory. They are alive in the unfolding elegance of knowledge and the rich institutions multiplying to grace our appetites for beauty and reflection. The legacy of intellectual gloom that grips academic men with other models and memories in mind ought to be finally dispelled. Moreover, the concerns that once worried C. P. Snow— the divisions among the scientific and humanistic cultures—have become sham battles, a collection of verbiage insensitive to the new collective power of professional knowledge.[17]

A leading American historian drives the point to its logical conclusion. The antifunctionalism of the humanists, the claims of cultural guardianship, compensated for the absence of felt power; the reactions against the "knowledge machine" and the "multiversity" have also been primarily compensatory mechanisms by which concerns about relative deprivation could be assuaged. In fact, the functional power of organized intellect in universities, government, and other organizations has realized the dream of potential intelligence. The whole professoriat—now powerful, privileged, and affluent—would not trade its public influence for the rhetorical maxims of the Enlightenment.[18] Even a sociologist critical of American academic and political life offers the candid observation that the currency of antifunctional critical knowledge may reveal more about the critics than the interlaced relations of men of knowledge and power in contemporary America.

Yet one cannot help feel that behind this concern [of unattached intellectuals] there often lurks an uneasy feeling that

[17]Lynn White, Jr., "On Intellectual Gloom," *The American Scholar,* 35:2 (1966), 223–226; John D. McKee, "The Great Academic Sham Battle," *The American Scholar,* 35:1 (1966), 197–207.

[18]John Higham, "The Schism in American Scholarship," *American Historical Review,* 72:1 (1966), 1–19. For a less strident account, note David Riesman, "Innovation and Reaction in Higher Education," in Arthur A. Cohen (ed.), *Humanistic Education and Western Civilization: Essays for Robert M. Hutchins* (New York: Crowell-Collier and Macmillan, Inc., 1964), pp. 182–205.

the literary man is no longer able to compete with the academic expert in terms of content. The specialized knowledge now available to the academic man, the statistical methods, quantifiable variables and complex research design he has at his disposal make the literary intellectual feel that he himself is on his way to obsolescence and that his technical incompetence paralyzes his capacity for insight.[19]

It remains for the social scientists to pave the middle ground, to articulate more fully the concepts appropriate to the public integration of functional knowledge, the modern university, and affairs of state. Modernizing the folkways of American society that William Graham Sumner had once found in the predatory strivings of a business ethos, Robert E. Lane articulates the folkways for a functionally mature knowledge-based society.[20] The function and expansion of knowledge creates power of its own usefulness in remedial policy changes. A likely state of affairs is a cycle encompassing the engagement of specific values by an awareness of new knowledge, its perculation among the policy professionals in government and the academy, and eventual application to cope with the social and psychological maladies of specific deprived groups. In a functional fit between academic and political man, university research team and governmental agency, knowledge and what is regarded as knowledge tends to be pervasive without explicit pressure groups to keep it publicly viable and without reference to an articulated forensic ideology. The social process of knowledge rather than appeals to the wisdom of the folk, the expertise of a specific elite, or the bonds among a beleaguered "community of scholars" itself increasingly influence the policy processes. No longer is it merely of academic importance that an objective truth criterion be among the basis of policy selection and that, in a knowledgeable society, knowledge must be public, its sources indicated, appeals to ideological premises and personal experience beyond the pale of operative policy formation.

The functional uses of the university, then, are more firmly grounded in social realism. The isolating and encapsulating ten-

[19]Lewis A. Coser, *Men of Ideas: A Sociologist's View* (New York: The Free Press, 1965), pp. 272–273.
[20]Robert E. Lane, "The Decline of Politics and Ideology in a Knowledgeable Society," *American Sociological Review,* 31 (October 1966), 649–662.

dency of institutional control are now more effectively countered by the public linkage among researchers and policy makers, among collegiate vocationalism and its corporate associates.

THE RISE OF VOCATIONALISM AND THE DECLINE OF PERSONAL KNOWLEDGE

The concept of the public vocational university means more than the commercial aspect of college life or the social utility of advanced degree. These internal tendencies are given political significance only in the context of the expanded relations between universities and the central government. The vocational university is a knowledge apparatus explicitly designed to create and apply ideas and personnel that are functional to dominant national policies. In external relations, the vocational university is dependent on federal and corporate public research interests, which in turn are sensitive to national foreign and domestic interests. In internal relations, both collegiate and intellectual patterns are replaced by cognitive vocationalism in which young men and women are trained for the needs of organized bureaucracies. More precisely, the new vocational universities have large numbers of first-college–generation students of lower-middle and working-class backgrounds. As an educational process, the applied research for national political interests is complemented by a curriculum and socialization process without much politically meaningful dialogue. In other words, the vocational university is modeled after the research and training institutes that have arisen since World War II. By effectively compartmentalizing applied governmental research and mass training (rather than education per se), the vocational university deceptively reflects a continuity with the Western cultural and political heritage. By contrast, the internal core of the liberal arts curriculum is the mastery over political events as well as subject matter through the cultivation of the rational and expressive faculties. Human concerns, not those of policy makers, are the core of education.

The forces of the liberal arts tradition extend deep in the Western tradition. The idea of knowledge for personal cultivation has been used to bolster the bourgeoisie's fight against aristocratic privilege, the Church's efforts to restrict the boundaries of truth, and the government's use of national security requirements as a means of curbing man's freedom. For instance, in the nineteenth-century orthodoxy of Cambridge University, education consisted of the traditional subjects' being repeated and refined but never advanced. The "newer sciences" such as physics and chemistry, based on the idea of creating new knowledge, found their entry into Cambridge blocked by conservative forces. Ironically, the disciplines that have since formed the core of modern scientific development were then regarded as too vocational and, as such, alien to the classical tradition. Thus, the dominant scientific and humanistic disciplines of the time fought the introduction of modern science into the Cambridge curriculum.[21]

In nineteenth-century America, the doctrine of personal cultivation applied to a distinct body of knowledge influencing religious practices or the social norms appropriate, as the case might be, for Southern gentlemen, Irish Catholics ascending from a segregated ghetto, or intellectuals in training.[22]

Moreover, the emphasis on personal cultivation sooner or later took up the question of character and the life style of educated men. Groups that felt their prestige and power slipping away could take refuge in the superiority of "gentle breeding," the proper forms and accents becoming the social panacea for the pretentions (*and* political power) of "uncultivated new men." Indeed, the current power of American knowledge and its inventive cadre has not gone uncriticized in the name of cultural taste. To Lewis Feuer, viewing the mass movements and administrative fluctuations at the University of California, education's goal of personal cultivation is not merely an objective to be seen as a product of student life:

The problem of the American intellectual class as it grows in power and numbers allied with the government, foundations, the publishing world, industry and the universities is that it demands for itself the prerequisites and prerogatives of a third chamber of government. It demands that government officials be eagerly accountable to it on the grounds of

[21]J. P. Powell, "Some Nineteenth Century Views on the University," *History of Education Quarterly*, 5:2 (1965), 97–109.

[22]The weight of cultural norms in a university's balance between a regional and national role is examined in Franklin L. Ford, "Our Universities: National and Regional Roles," *The Virginia Quarterly Review*, 43:2 (1967), 220–232.

intellect and knowledge. Yet it has scarcely shown itself to possess the character which its pretentions would require.[23]

To be sure, the goal of personal cultivation may find its roots in the democratization of human relations, the cultural amenities of an appointed (or self-appointed) clique, or in a reaction to the pace of institutional change as in "the romance of communitarianism." This latter tendency is reflected in the idealizing of the small college and the intimacies of face-to-face relationships among faculty and students.[24]

Yet more seriously, the liberalizing claims of education, claims for which there is not yet conclusive evidence, have often rested on the necessity of living in our technopolitical web; that is, the necessity to cultivate human sensitivities and capacities to deal with the by-products of the educational revolution itself.[25]

The achievement of new modes of comprehension and social arrangements to enhance human needs are major imperatives given the changing conditions of the knowledge-based society and its functional ways of life. While educational formalism strives for the democratization and expansion of talent, personal cultivation seeks to infuse quality and experience into the sprawling domains of cognitive knowledge. Indeed, as functional education stresses in monotonous detail an emphasis on the specialty, the profession, and the acquisition of skills useful for the expert monitoring of our political economy, the very expansion of education from the periphery to the center stage of American life has made the quest for personal commitment a more pressing concern.

It is in this context that the idea of a "living culture" that

---

[23]Lewis Feuer, "Reflections on Berkeley," *The Atlantic Monthly*, 218 (November 3, 1966), 87.

[24]For a critique of communal romanticism as a response to functional, modern educational systems, see Edgar Litt, *Studies in Politics and Civic Education* (Belmont, Calif.: Wadsworth Publishing Company, 1968), chap. 2.

[25]The individual gains of education in terms of problem-solving capacities, sense of political effectiveness, and tolerance of heterodox thought are well established, but the precise role of educational systems to these outcomes remains vague. The long-term problem is discussed by Martin Trow, "The Meaning of Impact," paper read at the Invitational Conference on Testing Problems, New York City, October 29, 1966. A succinct statement of the need for more personal capacity and empathy is Kenneth Kenniston, *The Uncommitted: Alienated Youth in American Society* (New York: Harcourt, Brace & World, Inc., 1964, chaps. 8, 9, 14.

will transmit group as well as individual tastes becomes a matter of critical urgency.[26] A society that will allocate high-quality educational opportunities to the few is content to use high myths and low mass distractions in order to ignore a creative culture. A society committed either to liberalizing individuals from the parochial boundaries of ethnicity and class or to utilitarian efforts adorned by cultural ornaments is too preoccupied to take personal cultivation as a serious educational matter. But a society whose intellectual and educational resources are central to its survival cannot afford to take the notion of personal cultivation so lightly.

In brief, the collective characteristics of the knowledge-based society make the university a critical microcosm of political and social development. Will the university liberate and educate publics or will to become a captive of the state? The massive scope, capsuled time schedules, and similarities to metropolitan culture reduce the opportunity for the shock of recognition that liberated individuals from more restricted orbits.[27] However, the emphasis on specialized, technical knowledge provides little guidance to experience, to sensitivity, or to such political arrangements as man from time to time may create. Beyond the search for identity and beyond participation in decisions affecting one's life situation, the personal significance of education lies in the effort to synthesize cognitive and affective learning, to synthesize the lifeways of the cultivated, educated man. It is the supreme irony that the difficulty and importance of this task are compounded by the instruments of the knowledge-based society itself. Men have fashioned lifeways in metropolitan cultures, specialized academies, and equalitarian state universities devoted to mass learning. But now the orbits of personal learning are precisely these structures of knowledge and technology supposedly constructed to liberate the human intellect. It is an ancient problem in modern guise; namely, the meaning of meanings to be commonly shared in the transactions of the new knowledge-based society.

[26]The "living culture" concept as an instrument of majority experience is used effectively by Raymond Williams, *Culture and Society: 1780–1960* (New York: Columbia University Press, 1960). For an insightful discussion of education's role in forming social values and culture, see Quinton Hoare, "Educational Progressivism and Man," *New Left Review,* 32 (July–August 1965), 40–52.

[27]The encounter between the small-town boy and the metropolitan university is a constant theme in David Riesman's writings on education; see, for instance, his *Constraint and Variety in American Education* (New York: Doubleday & Company, Inc., 1958), pp. 109–119.

Chapter 2
The Model Public Vocational University

Universities may expand and yet perform continuous services for a society. The processes of academic and civil learning may be extended to more people without fundamentally upsetting traditional expectations about the purposes of higher education. Or, universities may be seen in distinct spheres corresponding, for instance, to the functional, institutional, and cultural roles that were analysized in Chapter 1. Yet such possibilities account in only the most general way for the major transformations in American higher education during the last two decades.

An elitist or Marxist theory might stress the increases in stratification that have developed as part of the political integration in the higher learning. A romantic pluralism, seeking to comprehend new developments on the basis of past experiences, might stress the new diversities in student composition and academic purpose. The realities are much more complex than either of these partial views would suggest, yet they can be comprehended in the model of the national vocational university. This model of the university is less a transition from the parochial orbits of home and region than a microcosm of the complex political economy of American society. The national welfare university, with its assimilating and divisive strains, becomes a critical political institution whose implications extend beyond traditional notions of scholarship and "collegiate fun."

THE GROWTH OF THE PUBLIC SECTOR

The distinction between "public" and "private" universities is becoming less distinct as each becomes more influenced by the national culture and the federalism of federal fiscal policies. Moreover, the academic culture and social impact of a particular campus cannot be neatly divided by the formal affiliation of the institution. Yet despite these qualifications, the mutation in the public sector of American higher education is critical to an understanding of the political consequences in the social organization of learning. Equalitarians who would expand opportunities and reduce the "artificial" advantages of class and family have always placed great emphasis upon the duty of the public university to expand. In the progressive tradition, state universities enshrined middle-class utilitarianism, absorbed the imperatives of providing practical skills with those of cultural expansion, and served as the melting pots of diverse creeds and nationalities. Of more immediate practicality, the public universities have spawned major bureaucracies and created centers of influence for a new class of educational administrators; they have loomed large in the careers of governors and other governmental officials.

The plural nature of separate state systems endures, but it is overshadowed by powerful transforming forces. The first of these forces is the attendance growth rate in the public university.

In 1900, only 39 percent of all college students were enrolled in public colleges and universities. By 1960, 59 percent of all college students were enrolled in public universities. Of the 2100 colleges or universities in America today, about one-third are under state or local control—yet these educate about two-thirds of the nation's students! Analyzed in other terms, about fifty percent of all American college students attend public universities and state colleges and about twenty percent attend public junior colleges.[1] Projections by the American Council on Education suggest that fully 80 percent of all college students will be in public universities by 1985.[2]

The shift in attendance from private to public universities has been most dramatically demonstrated during the last two decades. in 1947, 50.4 percent of the total opening college enrollment was in the public sector; 49.6 percent was in the private sector. By 1965, 68.6 percent of all opening enrollments were accounted for by the public universities, while the private universities' share of the total enrollment had declined to 34.4 percent. The total collegiate enrollment was 3.6 million in 1960 and, according to American Council on Education estimates, it is expected to rise to 12.8 million by 1985. Based on these estimates, the public university sector will have absorbed about eighty percent of the growth in student population between 1960 and 1985. In other words, 8.1 million of the approximately 9.2 million new students to be educated by 1985 will be enrolled in public universities and colleges.

The recent dominance of public higher education is most visibly illustrated by the growth of the California university system, one of the leaders in American higher education. In 1921 only seven teacher colleges and thirty-five state colleges existed in California. By 1959 the pressure for new colleges had become so great that the state legislature appointed a special commission to evolve a master plan for higher education. The imperatives of modern society were reflected in the observation that "higher education had become the status symbol for the diverse Westerners, proof that every mountain or desert hamlet had culture, or at least knew some place close by where it could be had for the asking."[3] To create some order in a potentially chaotic situation, the commission, headed by Occidental College president Dr. Arthur G. Coons, evolved remedial legislation. Their master plan essentially

[1]Martin Meyerson, "The Ethos of American College Students: Beyond Protest," in Robert A. Goldwin (ed.), *Higher Education in the United States* (Skokie, Ill.: Rand McNally & Company, 1966), pp. 713–739.

[2]American Council on Education, Office of Statistical Information and Research, *A Fact Book on Higher Education,* Washington, D.C., April 1959 and May 1963.

[3]Mel Wax, "California Revolution 2: The Knowledge Bonanza," *The Nation,* 204:6 (1967), 179.

proposed a three-tier system of education rather than a unified establishment suggested by the governing board of education. Composed of universities, state colleges, and junior colleges, with specified academic duties and student clienteles for each group, the master plan effectively rationalized higher education if California. Since 1960, when the master plan was enacted, there have been 600,000 students in the junior colleges and 172,000 in the four-year state colleges. Overall, the California higher educational system has experienced a student growth rate of 10 percent, and that degree of expansion is forseen for the future.

The model public vocational university, the welfare state university, is large; it caters to a variety of utilitarian and esoteric interests, and it experiences the problems of complex administration and organization typical of large entities in this society. It provides the power of change and the rich diversity of skills required by a complex political economy. Yet it is as a microcosm of national political organization that the welfare state university has achieved a new significance. A purely functional view—a concept of university as training plant or skill processor—would not have these problems. For in the state-university system that was constructed after the land-grant college acts, pragmatic skills and liberalization from parochial cultures were demonstrable missions. But the public vocational university does more than equalize the working class through some degree of technical competence in accord with the new demands of government and industry. It reflects the strains of status and class that are particularly disturbing to cultural and social equalitarians, who viewed public education as the gateway to enhanced civic quality. While a classical elitist would wince at the flood of plebians and a Bismarckian administrator fret about the administrative problems, the equalitarian has hoped that college would offer a new experiential base for those previously denied higher academic opportunities.

The public vocational university by effectively replacing the class- or ethnic-based institution as mainstay of American education finds the reconciliation between quality and size and between cultural mission and functional necessity becoming the basis of its existence. Indeed, in disagreement with Clark Kerr's realistic view of the "multiversity" as all things to all men, it is more helpful to see the public vocational university as itself the testing ground for social and political arrangements. The combination of utilitarian skills and cultural sensibility that has been the hallmark of a middle-class view of general education are less appropriate to universities that profess to perform welfare functions for broader segments of the population. An educational system that is tied to the tradition of arts and literature characteristic of special cultural strata has now broadened its appeal and has now tied itself to the national political economy.

SOURCES OF STRATIFICATION

A national vocational university system is stratified in talent, resources, and opportunities. The degrees of stratification may be less crucial than the means used to cope with the enormous power-over-life chances that college education can confer. Students at colleges characterized by that "torpor at the tail of the procession"[4] do not compare the quality of their academic culture with that of Harvard and Haverford. However, it is precisely these isolated colleges that have been the recipients of federal attention devoted to improving their quality and performance. For instance, in 1966 the U.S. Office of Education sponsored a Coordination in Education agency designed to boost the teaching and research abilities of its twenty-six participating small colleges.[5] While a stratification fault line once divided the collegiate from the noncollegiate population, now it is the demarcations within the public university system that are of major importance. A systematic selection of college populations no longer tied to prior ethnic, cultural, or academic roots can most efficiently proceed when impersonal means are available to minimize discrepencies between achievement and aspiration and thus reduce the internal strains on the educational system as a major determinant of social position in later life.

Like the national welfare system in the political economy, the collegiate replica softens the contours of class, ideology, and skills. The process of stratification in the vocational university system is conveniently examined at the junior college level. Herein, failure for large numbers is structured within the rationalized

[4]David Riesman, *Constraint and Variety in American Education* (New York: Doubleday & Company, Inc., 1958), pp. 64–65.
[5]John Higham, "New Programs in Education," *School and Society*, 95:229 (1967), 174.

educational system rather than on its margins or in the conflicts of unassimilated social groups.[6]

As a "soft response" to the realities of specialization and educational stratification, alternative achievement is a realistic option to most junior college students. A series of techniques, such as emphasis on minute records, counseling as an agent of consolation, and gradual disengagement of the poor student from his aspirations toward advanced collegiate work, makes terminal students of those who might seek to transfer to other educational institutions. Of course, successful performance and transfer to advanced institutions also occurs, but the less visible terminal function of the junior college is important. Thus, the stratification of higher learning by different types of institutions and diverse categories of students meshes with the general welfare function of the public university in a national era.

Thus, in the California system the master plan encouraged academic (and indirectly, social) stratification by *type* of institution. The "top" 12.5 percent of the students from California high schools attend universities; the next 33.5 percent are in the state colleges; and the remainder are educated in the junior colleges. The stratification system is complemented by the unequal allocation of resources. Thus, the universities usually receive about fifty percent of state educational funds for teaching 37 percent of all the students, most of whom are not Californians, while the state colleges receive about forty-two percent of the state resources for teaching 62 percent of the students. Added prerequisites, such as sabbaticals, research facilities, and fringe benefits for faculties, are even more widely dispersed. Thus, while some see the junior, or community, college systems in terms of expanded opportunities for poor academic performers and members of minority groups, others note the relative deprivations and implicit "cooling out" function at the bottom of the system. As one junior college teacher lamented, "If what they want is some kind of social welfare program to keep the kids off the streets for two years after high school, okay. . . . [But] let's not call it a college and let's use social workers as teachers."[7]

---

[6]In the following analysis of the function of the junior colleges, I have drawn extensively on the brilliant analysis by Burton R. Clark, "The 'Cooling-out' Function in Higher Education," *American Journal of Sociology,* 65 (May 1960), 569–576.

[7]Quoted in Wax, "California Revolution 2," p. 179.

The general division of academic labor parallels the allocation of funds. By the terms of the 1960 master plan, the junior colleges were to provide terminal vocation and an Associate Arts degree for most students; the state colleges, most teachers and engineers and Master's degrees; and the universities, advanced graduate work and doctoral degrees.

Available evidence indicates lower self-evaluations held by junior college students as compared with all university students.[8] The drive to achieve leadership ability, mathematical ability, intellectual self-confidence, and writing ability are less abundant in the junior college population. The most outstanding distinction is the self-rating on academic ability: While only 36 percent of two-year college freshmen surveyed rated themselves above average, 61 percent of freshmen at four-year colleges (comprising 57 percent of freshmen at *all* institutions) and 69 percent of university freshmen responding to the study rated their academic ability above average.

The combination of broadened opportunity structure and intellectual leveling that characterizes the welfare university structure are evident in concerns other than their effects for stratification in American society. The dependence of the welfare university system on federal funds with its dominant allocation pattern has also significantly shaped the cultural and intellectual quality of the expanded American system of public higher education.

The interpenetration of industry, government, and the university has probably had its greatest effects on the public vocational university under public auspices. A participant observer describes the impact of the federal funding process:

> Federal support has become a major factor in the total performance of many universities, and the sums involved are substantial. Higher education in 1960 received about 1.5 billion dollars from the federal government—a hundredfold increase in twenty years. . . .
>
> This federal support has been almost exclusively identified with three great and somewhat inter-related national con-

---

[8]Comparisons are equally significant when junior college students are measured against freshmen from "all universities" or "all institutions"; see Alexander W. Astin, Robert J. Panos, and John A. Craeger, "National Norms for Entering College Freshmen," (Berkeley, Calif.: Center for the Study of Higher Education, Fall 1966 [mimeo]).

cerns: defense (40 percent of the total in 1961, including support by the Department of Defense and the Atomic Energy Commission); scientific and technological progress (20 percent—National Science Foundation, Department of Agriculture and NASA); and health (37 percent—through the National Institute of Health). Federal support has not been directed explicitly toward strengthening universities generally, or one or more universities specifically. . . .

Federal research expenditures have been largely restricted to the physical and biomedical sciences, and engineering with only about 3 percent for the social sciences and hardly any support for the humanities.[9]

Despite recent modifications, such as the establishment of an Institute for the Humanities, it is safe to say that the dominance of scientific contract research is matched only by the insignificant and insufficient funds spent on the quality of undergraduate education. The latter problem is most acute at those universities not in the high-quality research or private liberal arts elite. One informed estimate is that twelve universities receive more than 25 percent of all federal funds, while another 5 percent (encompassing about one hundred universities) receive most of the rest. Here, in fact, the functional uses of the university conflict with the cultural mission in the public vocational university.[10] The lockstep relationship of the public university to large-scale federal support to science and technology is seen in the finding that $1.6 million, or 10 percent of the total national budget, is allocated to research and development, most of it to research institutes within the universities.[11] "Despite the cries of alarm rising from faculty bars, transcontinental planes, and the cafeterias of the National Academy of Sciences," writes an expert on federal funding patterns, "science is still prospering."[12]

[9]Clark Kerr, *The Uses of the University* (Cambridge, Mass.: Harvard University Press, 1963), pp. 63–65.

[10]Meyerson, "The Ethos of American College Students"; Harold Orlans, *The Effects of Federal Programs on Higher Education* (Berkeley, Calif.: University of California Press, 1967).

[11]A. M. Weinberg, "Big Science: A Liability?" *Confluence*, 1 (Fall 1961), 1–5.

[12]Harold Orlans, "Developments in Federal Policy toward University Research," *Science*, 155 (1967), 666.

The federal role in higher education, especially in scientific and other research support, is accompanied on a smaller scale by the state governments. In twenty-six states for which general appropriations monies were available for the preceding three years, sixteen states showed a consistant increase in educational appropriations between 1959 and 1961. Moreover, percentage increases tended to be greatest for the most populous states, such as New York (20.1 percent) and Connecticut (24.6 percent). In 1961 approximately $237 million in bond issues earmarked for education was authorized in eighteen states. And in the welter of educational expansion at the two-year college level, 158 enactments dealing with two-year colleges were made by the states between 1956 and 1961.[13]

THE IMPACT OF CULTURES OF LEARNING

It would be foolhardy to suggest that either sheer growth or the federal funding of science, or even a combination of both developments, has retarded the cultural qualities of the public vocational university. Yet, a position less extreme than anarchism or political radicalism does tend toward cultural neglect of human resources. Despite current problems, the universities—especially public universities without cultural traditions to maintain—have not followed their responsibility to turn from self-concerns to an effective rebuilding and reorganizing of society. There is little evidence that much of the enormous federal funding has been constructively used by public vocational universities to turn man's empathic capacity toward a concern with social problems, to provide larger boundaries for testing experiences. A fair-minded judgment might be that our public colleges and universities have, with a few excellent exceptions, a long history of default on important social issues. They have sided with existing policies, not policies designed to help developing people. They have tied in with the powerful forces in government, law, and industry. They energetically carry on research with a powerful Department of Defense and other agencies that impede social change or conduct aggressive foreign policies.

[13]*Survey of State Legislation Relating to Higher Education,* Office of Education, U.S. Department of Health, Education and Welfare, Circular No. 684, OE 500008–61 (Washington, D.C.: Government Printing Office, 1962).

To a Tory such an observation is rather meaningless, for a Tory view of education is concerned with the mining of rare talent, not the wholesale effort to provide skills and culture in a mass society. Hence, the cultural and civic quality of the public vocational university becomes particularly important in the era of public dominance of higher education. The rationale of the public vocational university lies in its ability to contribute to the economic well-being of society and the social ascent of its students. The primary response, and often an effective response to custodians of liberal education, is that the model public university in the federal-grant era is the custodian of vocationalism. To be sure, there will always be an intellectual minority, but it is precisely the nationalizing tendencies of mass education that bind the public universities to vocational imperatives.

Moreover, the expansion of the welfare university in public higher education is accompanied by exposure to areas never before encountered in American universities. It is precisely the growth in technological power and the knowledge related to it that provides the milieu for the citizens of the national welfare university. While more integrated into the stratified knowledge system than ever before, the norms of cultural and civic sensibility and responsibility are particularly elusive.[14]

Especially at the public universities which lack the intellectual distinction or the ethos of a cultural group, the great conflict over the past fifty years has been between the academic and the collegiate subcultures; the former supported by the faculty and their allies in the professions and liberal public; the latter, by the football-inclined alumni and the great mass of uneducated, pragmatic citizens. Like the earlier conflict between science and religion, the conflict between the collegiate and academic realms becomes muted. Indeed, the complexity of large public universities has difficulty supporting the traditional collegiate subculture. For example, in the 1920s, campus newspapers were fragmented but often university-produced and collegiate in tune, emphasizing the variety of satire and local humor fashioned for adolescents. Today, the quality schools have a professional and socially conscious press, while the large public universities are seen, in culturally appro-

---

[14]The relationship between technology and symbolic transformation is discussed by Harvey Wheeler, "The Logic and Limit of Technology: Means, Ends, and Human Institutions," *The Nation*, 204:1 (1967), 9–16.

priate context, as an outlet for a campus version of the *Reader's Digest*. Designed to appear in college newspapers, *Campus Carrier* will appear once every two weeks during the school year, or sixteen issues per year. Forty pages, slick-papered, it will be entirely in color.[15]

The absence of a collegiate context is apparent in an era when education is important to national policy and the economy. By contrast, the conflict between vocationalism in the functional view of the public welfare university and impractical academic culture is quite genuine.[16] Neither the bogey man of federal funds nor malicious intent of the alumni association is to blame, although both are convenient villains. Rather, the combination of mass education, scientific ascendency, and encrusted institutional forms have resulted in a cultural lag, unrealistic to the demands of a complex society. When collegiate status was reinforced by peer expectations and academic norms, the cultural mission had a base of fairly secure initiates. When the typical university existed in cultural isolation, comparisons of quality and style were inhibited. However, the responsiveness of the public university to both multiple external interests as well as its own cultural and intellectual poverty contribute to the strains accompanying the current collegiate revolution.

First, there are the deep problems of status and identity, which is caused by rapid institutional expansion. One goes to college in a profoundly impersonal way without the bonds of a "subculture" that characterize established universities with genuine academic and social norms. In fact, the problems of size and scale—the inability of the average member to keep most of the campus and its actors in view—are aggravated by the absence of any cultural islands on the new campuses.

It is doubtful that you can find a single student among State University's 120,000 who think of themselves as attending the "State University of New York"; rather, he goes to Stony Brook or Cobbleskill, Oneida or Bronx Community. There is an undercurrent of disaffection, criticism, and even a

[15]John Tobbel, "Reader's Digest Goes to College," *The Saturday Review,* 232 (May 13, 1967), 92–93.

[16]Burton R. Clark and Martin Trow, "Determinants of College Student Subcultures," in T. Newcomb and E. Wilson (eds.), *College Peer Groups* (Chicago: Aldine Publishing Company, 1967), pp. 1–67.

kind of resigned bitterness among many SUNY students. "What will all these new buildings and new programs mean to me and my education?" asked a student in Buffalo State's newspaper. . . . Said a coed in the honors program at Albany, "This whole State University system seems mesmerized by the phrase 'one of the greatest universities in the nation.' "[17]

Yet, in the context of badly squandered educational opportunities under public auspices, the State University of New York was doing no more than responding to the imperatives of the vocational university. It has tripled its enrollment since 1948 and has launched on a gigantic program of physical expansion that will require $1.5 billion by 1971. It has averaged a new community college per year for the past five years, and the pace is due to be stepped up. Two more four-year colleges are in the planning stage, scheduled to open in 1970. Three complete new campuses are now being built—at Stony Brook on Long Island, at Binghamton in south-central New York, and at Albany—with a number of others, including two new medical centers, planned. In this context, the interpersonal sensitivities of *communitas* seem patently illusory.

Yet it is not merely the factors of growth and size that underlie the transformation of the public vocational university. The strains of functionalism include the lower-middle-class base of the mushrooming student population and the vocational choices that often dominate in the public university. The major undergraduate increases in vocational choices are in engineering, education, business, and other "majors" with an uncertain foundation of intellectual content. For instance, in the fall of 1965, more than half of all New York State University's undergraduates (outside the two-year colleges) were enrolled in professional and education programs. The 28,000 enrolled in education compared with only 12,000 in arts and sciences, and with another 28,000 enrolled in business, engineering, and a variety of other professional programs. In the ex-teachers' colleges, the proportion of students enrolled in education programs was overwhelming—in most instances upward of 90 percent.

[17]Ronald Gross and Judith Murphy, "New York's Late-Blooming State University," *Harper's,* 233 (1966), 94.

In the nation as a whole during the years between 1954 and 1958, vocational curricula—business administration, engineering, and education, which account for nearly half of all undergraduate degrees—grew nearly twice as fast as the total number of college graduates: The number of degrees earned in these fields increased by 49 percent as compared with an increase of 27 percent in all Bachelor's and Master's degrees. By 1962, however, enrollment in business and engineering remained relatively static, and only education, of these three fields, continued to grow rapidly. Indeed, later, in the 1960s, engineering enrollment dropped steadily.[18] However, the vocational subjects had their main strength within the large public universities and its supporting networks of state and junior colleges.

While qualifications are important, there appears to be a reinforcing relationship among large-scale vocationalism, and the atomization of activities that support welfare university functionalism. As Clark and Trow suggest:

> The tendency for increasing size to weaken social ties, turning groups into aggregations, leads toward the atomized vocational subcultures. Conversely, vocationalism encourages growth in size and complexity. Business association, professional bodies, and other interest groups that see the college as a training center encourage colleges to proliferate occupational curricula; students mindful of upward mobility seek occupational preparation in a host of fields. Occupational training in a complex society is indeed efficiently handled by large enterprises tooled to train large numbers in diverse fields.[19]

These realities direct our attention to the network of interpersonal relations among students and faculty. The root of the "cultural mission" concept is that self-concepts and cognition are bolstered and that the qualities of civility are taught in faculty-student dialogue. In fact, it is usually when in addition to specific studies students are exposed to a relatively homogeneous sup-

[18]Percentages are from the American Council of Education, *A Fact Book on Higher Education,* April 1959–June 1966.
[19]Clark and Trow, "Determinants of College Student Subcultures," p. 46.

porting atmosphere that education is strongly related to later social and political choices.[20]

Now multiple reference groups are available among peers, those faculty members who support intellectual qualities, the social and esthetic culture of the campus. Herein the abilities to balance opinions and cultivate judgments can be enhanced. However, in the functionalism of the model public university, the schism between vocationalism and sociocultural concerns may be enormous. In order to increase the tolerance of diverse opinions that characterizes intellectual liberalism, there must be exposure to diverse opinions and patterns of belief. At least the "cultural mission" thesis encourages generalized liberalism, those flexibilities of mind and judgment that comprise the educated man. The growth of tolerance can be found in functionalism too, a willingness to appraise the evidence and make realistic judgments within the confines of the speciality. Yet it is more its application than its nature that is relevant to the public vocational university.

The cumulative evidence supports, with important complexities, the belief that formal education enhances participation, tolerance of ideas, intellectuality, and the absence of mental rigidity. Yet these impacts have been found most often and with greatest intensity among the student leaders at high-quality colleges and universities, especially those in the social science and humanities fields.[21] These are not the groups now inundating the public universities. The floodgates could be closed by tightening the admissions processes, raising the standards of academic excellence to be demanded, formalizing academic discourse so as to make the bridge

---

[20]The leading case in point, possible because it is one of the few studies of "college socialization" followed over time, is that of Bennington College. See Theodore M. Newcomb, *Personality and Social Change: Attitude Formation in a Student Community* (New York: Holt, Rinehart and Winston, Inc., 1943); Alex S. Edelstein, "Since Bennington: Evidence of Change in Student Political Behavior," *Public Opinion Quarterly,* 26 (Winter 1962), 564–577.

[21]Key studies include Honon C. Selvin and Warren Hagstrom, "Determinants of Support for Civil Liberties," *British Journal of Sociology,* 11 (March 1960), 51–73; Herbert Hyman, *Political Socialization* (New York: The Free Press, 1959); V. O. Key, Jr., *Public Opinion and American Democracy* (New York: Alfred A. Knopf, 1961), pp. 315–343; Paul Heist, "Intellect and Commitment "(Berkeley, Calif.: Center for the Study of Higher Education, 1967 [mimeo]).

between it and the "public" language of the middle mass un-fathomable.[22]

But the equalitarian creed and the expansion of opportunities it supports run counter to the functional impetus of the public welfare university. Herein lies the political significance of the national welfare university in its era of expansion. For it is precisely among the middle mass in the enlarged public universities that the cultural (and possibly, political) mission of higher education faces its most severe test. Available studies portray effective socialization (allegiance to the American system, party choice of parents) and absence of political content (concern about issues, knowledge of the Bill of Rights, contextual participation and awareness of its limitations and consequences).[23] Neither a glorification of the system-maintaining common man nor abstract hymns to the un-limited power of education are consonant with these realities.

To be sure, there are the teachers, but specialization and functionalism reduce their potential effectiveness. Moreover, teachers can become anxious by a political crisis threatening their scholarly work, project feelings of low esteem and hostility onto political matters, and carefully divide political participation between the "external" (and more permissive) and "internal" (and less permissive) classroom situation.[24]

[22]The political implications of language in educational institutions are in the work of Basil Bernstein; for instance, "Some Sociological Determinants of Perception," *British Journal of Sociology,* 9 (June 1958), 159–174, and "Family Role Systems, Sources and Communications," paper presented at the Conference on Cross-Cultural Research into Childhood and Adolescence, University of Chicago, Chicago, Ill., 1964.

[23]See Russell Middleton and Shelden Putney, "Political Expression of Adolescent Rebellion," *American Journal of Sociology,* 68 (1963), 527–535; Jack Dennis, "Support for the Party System by the Mass Public," *American Political Science Review,* 60 (September 1966), 600–615; Robert E. Lane and David Sears, *Public Opinion* (Englewood Cliffs: Prentice-Hall, 1964), chap. 6.

[24]See P. F. Lazarsfeld and W. Thielens, Jr., *The Academic Mind* (New York: The Free Press, 1958); see also, Harmon Zeigler, *The Political World of the High School Teacher* (Englewood Cliffs, N.J.: Prentice-Hall, Inc., 1967), especially the discussion of the status-frustrated male teacher. A sensitive account of psychological needs expressed in the teaching act is Joseph Katz's "Personality and Interpersonal Relations in the College Classroom," in Nevitt Sanford (ed.), *The American College: A Psychological and Social Interpretation of the Higher Learning* (New York: John Wiley & Sons, Inc., 1962), pp. 365–395.

Moreover, the marginal stimulants of intellectual or scholarly self-definition are less pervasive in the teaching corps of the public welfare university. The gains of power and status are weighted against the loss of energetic militancy when, as is no longer the usual case, the adjoining community were philistines shocked by the political and social style of academic types. Along with the absence of risk taking that characterizes mature institutions comes that social leveling and day-to-day professional class competence of the assimilated academic men. It is in the context of cultural enlightenment that criticisms of the mature reality are most usefully viewed. For instance, the impoverished self is a synoptic concept with which to comprehend the combination of psychological factors producing the undemocratic citizen.[25] In the same spirit, the avoidance of general ideas or their displacement in the vocabulary of specialized expertise are prominent in a critical appraisal of the graduate training to meet, in no small measure, the demands of the public vocational university: These students who are destined to become the integrated intellectual servants of society are persuaded to exchange their previous motivations and concern about general ideas for the dynamics of work puritanism.[26]

Indeed, the social gains of educational functionalism may also be countered by an aversion to critical intellect, particularly in the public vocational universities. Along with broadened professionalism may come some less noble effects of expanded opportunity, effects that reinforce the functional neutrality of the public vocational university. Such academic lowbrows have contempt for intellectuals. Their pet peeves are the terms "intelligentsia," "highbrow," "profound"; while their major positive terms are "valuable," "interesting," and "productive." Immune to learning and the discussion of ideas, the academic plebe supports the denaturing of the social sciences and humanities and the advance of science and applied technology. He views the most important university function as that of efficient management and the best educational policy as that of widening the range of activities and personnel. Accepting the prevailing programs of the community, he either views criticism as out of bounds or more often reinforces

[25]Robert E. Lane, *Political Ideology: Why the American Common Man Believes What He Does* (New York: The Free Press, 1962), pp. 409–412.
[26]J. MacDonald, "The Topmost Layer: An Examination of the Structure and Fortunes of American Graduate Schools," *Comparative Education*, 2:3 (1966), 155.

the dominant role of neutral technician. The most important objective which is sought by the academic lowbrow is the achievement of a conventional respectability. He therefore perceives the image of a university as a collection of Rotarians, Shriners, and Elks each of which might be your next door neighbor.[27]

The irony of these cumulative developments in the eyes of a democratic equalitarian (one who supports the expansion of educational opportunities) is that a knowledge-based society especially requires the cultivation of intellectual sensitivity and political competence not normally found or fostered among the majority of neophyte citizens in the public welfare university.

Proposals for reform are more easily made than implemented; "innovation" and "change" have about them the warm connotation of fashionable terms. Nevertheless, in the context of the public welfare university, one major (and not very costly) institutional change is useful and practical. The economics of seminars and individualized instruction as well as the political realities of guild veto among dominant interest groups vitiate the kind of structural reform that flow from the pen of the latest academic radical. Yet a student research center devoted to the exploration of human growth and development seems a useful element of genuine political and liberal educational policy. Combining the skills of social research with the concerns of relevant students (these are likely to focus on youth culture, peace, civil rights), it could provide some institutional linkage between the consumership of youth culture and the structured realities of the state welfare university. Particularly at institutions lacking the viable culture of academic excellence or sociological distinctiveness, such an endeavor ought to replace the student union (the shopping plaza for young adults in consumer training) as the physical and intellectual center of the public university in the middle rank.

The idea of the public university as a political microcosm in a knowledge-producing society requires the subtle blending of social, psychological, and political resources. In a society where class and ethnic differences were great, the college plaza and the coffeehouse were meaningful centers in which to cope with interpersonal relations. But at a time when the production of social knowledge and institutions that are geared to the training of relevant skills

---

[27]Henry Winthrop, "The New Know Nothings in Education," *The Colorado Review*, 101 (June 1966), 226.

dominates the academic landscape, the center of undergraduate learning ought to be of appropriate scale and purpose, ideally student-run and closely geared to the study of problems in adjoining communities. It is this union of cognitive and affective learning, of social concerns and academic forms that most markedly would change the less attractive features of the public universities now bloated by the functional requirements of external interests and the concomitant demands of parental and student pressures.

Chapter 3
Countercyclical Policies in the Public Vocational University

To single-minded critics the public vocational, or welfare state, university is a hodgepodge of inconsistencies demanding reform. The irrationality of bureaucracies, the supression of ideas by anti-intellectual teachers, and the training of students to instant obedience before authority are some of the university's shortcomings. Yet it is the scope of the new higher learning and its role in the political economy that reveal the inadequacies of these criticisms. If Paul Goodman found the enormity of the administrative scale depressing, it is the scope of the public universities that have facilitated the academic "leveling up" of previously excluded minority groups.[1] If Edgar Friedenberg discovered that lower-middle-class resentment inhibits adolescent growth, the public universities

[1] Paul Goodman, *The Community of Scholars* (New York: Random House, Inc., 1962); Edgar Friedenberg, *The Vanishing Adolescent* (New York: Random House, Inc., 1966); Jules Henry, "Docility or Giving Teacher What She Wants," *Journal of Social Issues,* 2 (1955), 33–41.

have made available new opportunities that reduce social-class distinctions. If Jules Henry found that docility to authority is the prime quality of classroom activity, the young are also aware that the vocational welfare university allocates skill credentials for society.

Nevertheless, the welfare state university is perhaps more open to criticism in the culture of a knowledge-based society than in more blatantly anti-intellectual periods. The public university effectively blends the new affluence of the lower-middle-class with the expanded demands of federal and corporate activities. It is this common denominator as purveyor of goods and services that shapes the political role of the welfare university. That role is based upon the rapid acculturation of student masses to the requirements of a complex political economy.

This functionally smooth socialization process, a view of the university solely as the site for grooming to job and marriage, would be particularly impressive if the human costs were small. One might expect the pipedreams of intellectuals or the sensitivities of affection-seeking young men to reflect these costs.[2] However, the evidence of human costs in the new educational functionalism is not limited to such groups. For instance, as reported in the three studies by Stern, replies from 2075 freshmen enrolled in three very different schools (Beloit, a private liberal arts college; Cazenovia, a junior college for women; and St. Louis, a Catholic, urban university) indicate that more than three-fourths of the students in these four incoming classes believed that their schools expected them "to develop a strong sense of responsibility about their role in contemporary social and political life" and that this would not only involve "developing ideals but also expressing them in action."[3]

[2]Note Jacques Barzun, *The House of Intellect* (New York: Harper & Row, Publishers, 1959); Henry D. Aiken, "What Is a Liberal Education?" *The New York Review of Books* (November 3, 1966), 23–29; Robert E. Lane, "The Need to Be Liked and the Anxious Liberal," *The Annals of the American Academy of Political and Social Science,* 361 (September 1965), 32–39.

[3]G. G. Stern, *Scoring Instructions and College Norms: Activities Index, College Characteristics Index* (Minneapolis: National Computer Systems, 1963); G. G. Stern, *Studies of College Environments* (Syracuse, N.Y.: Psychological Research Center, 1966); G. G. Stern, "Myth and Reality in the American College," *American Association of University Professors Bulletin,* 52:4 (1966), 408–413.

These freshmen also thought that other students and faculty were going to be "actively concerned about national and international affairs," that a "number of prominent professors play a significant role in national or local politics," and that, as students, they would be "encouraged to take an active part in social reform and political programs . . . the expression of strong personal beliefs and political programs being far from rare here." An even higher percentage of the freshmen believed that "no one needs to be afraid of expressing extreme or unpopular viewpoints in this school," since it "has an excellent reputation for academic freedom" and that "the values most stressed here are open-mindedness and objectivity." It is interesting to note, however, that barely half of the seniors at these colleges agreed with these statements.

These findings provide little support for the view that the incoming freshman's expectations for the college he has just entered are either cynical, indifferent, or dissolute. On the contrary, he brings with him to college a naïve, enthusiastic, and boundless idealism concerning his chosen college's ways and purposes. This view was not generated out of prior learning or the predispositions of the students. Unlike the culturally enriched minority that enter elite liberal arts colleges, most freshmen's expectations of what the university is supposed to be like come from the viewpoints of friends, families, and high school counselors.

The new student arrives with great expectations, reinforced by everyone save the curiously cynical upperclassmen or faculty member whom he is not likely to know anyway. Undergraduate students in large universities, in particular, must be disappointed both about the qualities of intellectualism and the institutional supports for communal organization. Their most viable institutional option is to fall back upon the broad opportunities for student play available in the adolescent collegiate mold—in fact, one of the lesser expectations of these freshmen. This hard empirical evidence confirms the impressions of one "utopian critic," namely that "the youth culture as only a reaction to interrupted growing up, is against the consensus."[4]

What, then, are the alternatives to the type of functional socialization that can be provided by the national vocational university? For it is the absence of some sense of transition, some

[4] Paul Goodman, *The Community of Scholars* (New York: Random House, Inc., 1962), p. 109.

clarification of self in relation to choices, that most reinforces anti-intellectualism within these institutions. Five options that do not include a dismembering of existing institutions appear relevant. The political meaning of the national vocational university lies in its reflection of the American political culture. The university is a political microcosm in which efforts to provide the richness of an elite culture to many will be played out. Neither the rejection of scale (a romance of communitarianism that avoids the broad base of contemporary education) nor radical reconstruction (including the advocacy of a particular political ideology) aims at the difficult task of balancing functional necessity and cultural quality.

THE TOTAL INSTITUTION

The first option is a complete resocialization that will counter student withdrawal or exclusion. The problem at hand is the social isolation of those who cannot find a proper credentials-granting institution among the many and varied American colleges and universities. In the mainstream of the national vocational university, this problem is more likely to concern the large number of inept students, rather than the minority cadre of students seriously interested in ideas.[5] The fulfillment of "national needs," which requires productive college graduates, effectively excludes the play of cognitive and affective knowledge. Despite national dropout rates, which average about forty percent of all entering freshmen in 1962, the logic behind the total-institution concept is that there is a college for everyone, a gradually reduced scale of academic demands and subsequent social rewards. Increasingly, withdrawal or dropout represents a failure in the core value of collegiate attainment, an indication that the dropout is a nonfunctional member of a knowledgeable society.

Martin Meyerson, now chancellor of the State University of New York, speaks eloquently of the personal basis of academic failure:

At the same time that students need greater intellectual guidance, perhaps moral guidance as well, the more appar-

[5]See William Goode, "The Problem of the Inept," *American Sociological Review*, 32 (February 1967), 5–19.

ent it becomes that the students are poorly prepared by professional contact, less affected by adult contact, less time is spent with professors beyond classes and office hours. . . . The more I met with different students, the more I realized that they were not so much objecting to classes as much as to general neglect.[6]

The system of stratification within the evolving public vocational university makes the perception of failure an individual matter that is internalized rather than expressed against the political structure of the educational system. The most obvious corrective in this situation is *resocialization,* ideally within a total institution that ministers to the multiple problems of the new custodians of the welfare university apparatus. In the broadest terms, the problem of failure in a system granting such wide options for individual opportunity becomes a political issue.

Intensive personal education for distinct minorities (authoritarian students, racial groups, working-class youth who lack academic skills) is one of the concrete meanings of the term "community" so often encountered in the literature of educational criticism. However, there are two important objections, one of substance and one of implementation, to total resocialization as a broad public policy.

The substantive criticism is that resocialization concentrates unusually large amounts of educational resources among intense minorities by effectively segregating students. The germinating idea may have evolved from class-conscious elite schools, but there are no present guidelines to proper guardianship within intense communities on a mass scale. This effective segregation may, in fact, isolate the individual, encourage the covert indoctrination of specific beliefs, and yield a collective product that cannot cope with civil society. The resocialization strategy often removes individuals from extensive contact with others in order to make them more aware of their social roles. Thus, prisons, mental hospitals, and classes for remedial learning are examples of some resocializing agencies. However, the racially segregated college designed to instruct Negroes about their "proper" place in society,

[6]Martin Meyerson, "The Ethos of the American College Student: Beyond Protest," in Robert A. Goldwin (ed.), *Higher Education in the United States* (Skokie, Ill.: Rand McNally & Company, 1966), p. 731.

the military training program designed to discard personal identity as an obstacle to effective performance as a professional soldier, the job-training program that seeks to teach skills supposedly unlearned because of a crippling environment—these are more recent examples of total resocialization programs.[7]

The tendency is to encourage extreme dependency upon overt authority, to constrict the role models available for inspection, and to increase the power of secretive and exploitive forces that would mold young men in their own image. In reality, resocialization has often meant the training of young men to kill, the inculcation of distrust and the tactics of the political voyageur. Weighted heavily against those ameliorating social programs designed to restore self-esteem and personal adequacy are the legacies of the Cold War, with its networks of espionage and militarism, in which resocialization becomes yet another way of legitimizing the power of the state.

The second objection to resocialization as a comprehensive strategy concerns implementation and limited application. Resocialization agencies have only limited resources for dealing with the "normal" problems of mass student and complex-organizational life. Since these are the pervasive realities of the higher learning, intensive concentration upon the cultural needs of the few leaves untouched the basic human needs of the student upon whom the public vocational university structures most heavily depends. Therefore, resocialization becomes a special-problems approach, with emphasis on the education of a particularly gifted or particularly disadvantaged minority. Such particularism is least suited to the broad cultural and intellectual malaise of the knowledge-based society.

ADJUSTMENTS OF SIZE AND SCALE

A second option is an institutional adjustment that is designed to provide some support against the consensus of the vocation-oriented public university. Established variations of this option

[7] S. N. Dornbusch, "The Military Academy as an Assimilating Institution," *Social Forces,* 33 (May 1955), 316–321; Robert Lifton, "Youth and Hostility: Individual Change in Postwar Japan," *Daedalus,* 91 (Winter 1962), 172–197; Urie Bronfenbrenner, "Soviet Methods of Character Education," *American Psychologist,* 17 (Winter 1962), 550–564.

range from independent study and honors programs to more comprehensive plans for restoring a sense of human scale in the cluster and experimental colleges. The central objectives of these variations are to make size and scale more comprehensible and to strengthen the academic culture by grounding it in primary-group interaction. The "cluster college" concept and others like it are most likely to have their greatest impact on the more talented members of the next generation's leadership class, who are found at those institutions where there already exists a viable academic culture:

> The problem of the superior student at upper middle-class and upper-class academic institutions [does not include] an intensive drive for material advancement, social elevation or personal development. By and large, he already has it "made." Attendence at college for him is often merely a function of his class. He goes to college because everyone he knows goes to college and it would be unthinkable for him not to do so. For some such, the campus is perceived as a theatre in which the student is one of the actors with a role to play and a script to follow. He thinks of what he does as a "performance," and, in public, he is always on guard or on stage. Teachers and students are sets of actors in the same production, separated, literally, by the prosenium of the platform or the desk. The object of the role is the successful presentation. Marks, grades, and other signs of approval constitute the scores by which gains and losses are counted by the student player. These are the campus equivalents of the critics' notices in which dramatic productions live or die.[8]

However, the varieties of institutional adjustments do not touch the bulk of students from the lower-middle and working classes who swell the burgeoning vocational universities. A less demanding view of higher education, a contentment with the vo-

[8]Earl Latham, "The Superior Student," in Robert Connery (ed.), *Teaching Political Science: A Challenge to Higher Education* (Durham, N.C.: Duke University Press, 1965), pp. 155–156. Note also the critical review of studies on the relation between effective teaching and class size by Robert H. Connery, "Now Bring Together," in Connery (ed.), *Teaching Political Science*, pp. 238–265.

cational skills to be offered and later applied, would make one satisfied with the academic outcomes. But a creative strata of American educators and intellectuals has often promised at least some effort to enlarge the orbits of cultural sensitivity and political awareness. It is this heritage among the elite and avant garde colleges spawned by the Progressive movement that is on the line in the welfare university's monumental growth.

As the Progressive movement sought to arrest and humanize the industrial expansion a half century ago, so currently some educators attempt to restrain size and depersonalization in colleges. The most recent and imaginative countervailing policies in this effort are to be found in the cluster-college concept. Most widely inaugurated at the new University of California in Santa Cruz, but also evident in university planning from the University of Massachusetts to the University of Kansas, the emphasis is on small units of students and faculty in residence following some special interest, usually in the social sciences and the humanities.[9] It is too early to assess the impact of these efforts, but it would be unrealistic to expect more than marginal increments in the cultural and personal bases of established large universities.

The cluster-college concept is designed to alter the institutional arrangements in order to provide more varied educational experiences. Its success depends on the efficacy of tutorial models, adapted from European and private education, to the raw expanses of American universities. By intentionally maximizing social proximity of students and faculty, the cluster-college architects have been guided by earlier periods of university development. Although these academic republics-in-miniature may intensively influence the life styles of some students, the critical resources of talent and funds are flowing to other parts of the knowledge industry.

Another obstacle to successful academic innovation is the physical structure of the public vocational university. The college of the past seventy-five years is particularly ill-suited and essentially inimical to supportive restraints against the consensus of vocationalism. Its basic organizational structures—grades, credits, and fragmented courses—reflect its dedication to instrumental

[9]Paul Woodward, "The Small College on the Big Campus," *The Saturday Review* (January 21, 1967), 64–69.

learning as a preparation for something else. But the virtues of discipline and unmodified vocationalism are no longer quite so evident.

The idea of academic islands, however implemented, also fails to raise the critical political problem of individual capacity for adaptation to rapid social change. There is more than a modicum of truth to the critiques of social radicals, who claim that institutional blandness encourages the self-concepts of the neutral technician in a period when human adaptation to organizational structures is a major concern. One underlying reason for the absence of "learned" political participation is the incongruity between motives to participate and the organizational realities of educational systems.[10]

The limitations of countervailing modifications within large universities also stem from the legacies of past educational planning. For instance, university-planning politics at large universities are often predicated on existing facilities and anticipated growth rates. With committees often dominated by scientists and engineers, the major capital-improvements schedule reflects, in a not uncommon political process, the interests of established institutional agencies. Thus, at the University of California in Berkeley, a university with much greater intellectual and political concerns than the typical public vocational university, of the $142 million in major improvements for directly academic use requested for 1968 to 1973, $136 million was for sciences, professional schools, and institutes.[11] Only $4 million was requested for alterations in some of the humanities buildings, and only $1.8 million was requested for library alterations. Of the $38.8 million which the campus might conceivably get from the state of California, $10

[10]On the meaning of operative political curriculum in urban schools, see Edgar Litt, *Studies in Politics and Civic Education,* (Belmont, Calif.: Wadsworth Publishing Company, 1968).

[11]"Report on campus planning," made for the faculty-student Study Commission on University Governance and published in *The Daily Californian,* 194:27 (1967), 6–7. In summary data for entering freshmen, 91.8 percent of Berkeley freshmen rated themselves above average in academic ability and 68.0 percent rated themselves above average on intellectual self-confidence. Corresponding "high" self-evaluations for all university freshmen were 22.4 percent and 43.1 percent. (Office of Research, American Council on Education, Washington, D.C., Fall 1966). Campus planning at Berkeley is not designed for the social and intellectual needs of its talented, nonvocational students.

million was allocated for administration, general campus improvements, and utilities, while $28.4 million was for direct academic use.

The sciences, engineering, and professional schools are scheduled to receive $26.7 million, while the institutes will get $0.80 million and the library will get $0.90 million. In effect, the social sciences, humanities, and fine arts can expect to get no major capital improvements in the next five years unless they have already been funded. Concluded the report of the faculty-student Study Commission on University Governance:

> The wholly disproportionate allocation to the sciences does not mean that the humanities do not need facilities. . . . the humanities were especially lacking adequate library and graduate study facilities. On studying the *Requests,* it would seem that humanities requests are given only token consideration by placing them so low in priority that there is little chance they will be granted. For instance, History and Dramatic Art have both requested remodeling. . . . The proposed remodeling is the most inexpensive of the 91 proposed projects, but is ranked 76th in priority, insuring that it will be impossible. The other four humanities requests are numbers 31, 33, 36, and 82 respectively—all well below what can be expected to be granted.[12]

The normal pattern in which long-range planning for university expansion occurs is often at a level unaccountable to those who use the facilities of the public vocational university.

CREATING AN EXPERIENTIAL BASE

A third option is to conceive of the university as the experiential base for testing ideas and practices germane to a liberalizing education. That such opportunities exist widely in American universities is quite evident. That they exist in the rich profusion required by the institutional logic of the public vocational university is hardly evident. It is precisely the middling citizens of the public

[12]"Report on Campus Planning," p. 7.

vocational university who are most responsive to institutional adaptations that foster their own initiative.[13]

In fact, the growth of specialized study, faculty research, and the mass student base of the public university increase the need for combining self-learning with educational esthetics. Ideally, in an era of unprecedented knowledge output, these esthetics correspond to the core ways of knowing phenomena. Pondering the role of general education in a functionally specialized educational system, Daniel Bell suggests that the indispensible education which a liberally endowed university college alone can adequately provide should be a continuous, increasingly sophisticated training in the methods of inquiry and learning which the natural sciences, the social sciences, and the humanities respectively exemplify.[14] In Bell's account, the strategy characteristic of mathematics and the natural sciences are supposedly sequential or linear, moving from axioms to theorems, from hypotheses to their deducible consequences, and from simpler ideas and subject matters to those that are more complex. In the social sciences, on the other hand, both inquiry and learning are conceived in terms of linkages in which the understanding of one kind of phenomenon (for example, economic characteristics of the vocational university administration) cannot be contained and is possible only by an understanding of linked contexts (for example, the vocational student's role within a social system). In the humanities, the method of knowledge is conceived of as concentric in which constant use is made of central themes, such as self-discovery and the nature of tragedy.

The critical application of Bell's thesis is the fusion of core intellectual strategies within their institutional context in the university. The culture of the university is created in human drama, social experimentation, and scientific investigation, and uses the institutional base as a primary field of inquiry. I recall a "power study" of one university in which deference to authority and the avoidance of social inquiry were important features of the collegiate culture. One consequence of even such a small effort as this study

---

[13]See Litt, *Studies in Politics and Civic Education,* chap. 6.

[14]Daniel Bell, *The Reforming of General Education* (New York: Columbia University Press, 1967). The emphasis on cognitive comprehension in a society where direct personal experience is inadequate is also found in Solon T. Kimball and James E. McClellan, Jr., *Education and the New America* (New York: Vintage Books, Random House, Inc., 1962), esp. chap. 11.

was a fresh perception of the different expectations held about interpersonal and academic relations among the faculty and students in the college.

Moreover, the combination of epistemology and the institutional base within the public vocational university provides meaning to the natural learning claims of an earlier educational progressivism. Harold Taylor, former president of Sarah Lawrence, makes the claim for student-initiated inquiry in these terms:

> The reason for shifting the entire pedagogy away from lecturing toward discussion and independent study is that discussion and independent enquiry are the natural and the most effective ways to learn. They do not require the continual presence of the teacher or any kind of educational authority to be effective. The students discuss all the time anyway; it is a question of how to get them discussing matters of significance to their higher education and of teaching them how to get the most out of discussion and enquiry. The real problem is to teach them how to teach each other and how to learn from each other, from books, from experience, from their teachers, from anything.[15]

Yet, without help from innovative professionals willing to explore the institutional base for signs of political and cultural life, such student participation may become an unstructured search for substance. Taken seriously, a clinical approach is fruitful in which professional staffs (faculty, researchers, and clinicians) provide guidelines to such inquiries. Proposal flows from the pragmatic realities of size and specialization within the national vocational university, circumstances that usually curtail widespread student-initiated studies. It also takes cognizance of the vocational restraints upon successful students who partly direct their own education. In fact, professional staffs (possibly located in undergraduate centers) provide the most continuous and sizeable resources for developing relationships among the forms of knowledge and their application in the university.

[15]Harold Taylor, "Comments on the Improvement of Teaching," in *Education at Berkeley, Report of the Select Committee on Education,* University of California, Berkeley Academic Senate, March 1966, pp. 44–45.

UTILIZATION OF EXTERNAL SUPPORTS

A fourth option to the vocational leveling within the national welfare university draws on those external student activities that liberate human behavior. There seems little reason for not incorporating the external experiences of social and political learning into the national welfare university. In fact, the failure to see the extention of human contact in social and political activism by students as a potentially critical learning experience has contributed to the compartmentalization of academic studies and psychological impact. The institutional defaults of the public vocational university do not auger well for its socially responsible role as custodian of a knowledge-based society.

> The big universities . . . have become corporations for the producing, transmitting, and marketing of knowledge, and in the process have lost their intellectual and moral identity. At the time that they should have been creative centers for the development of strategies for peace, disarmament and world unity, they were busy with defense department contracts. When the educational problems of the Negro were getting worse by the day, they were busy making admission requirements more and more favorable to the white middle-class students from privileged environments. When the social habits and material ambitions of the citizens were following the lead of the advertising agencies, the universities were producing graduates whose intellectual equipment was suited to reading advertising copy. When the public schools were groping for ways of improving the intellectual content of their curriculum, the universities were sneering at teachers colleges and schools of education as the province of the intellectually unfit and the spiritually slothful. At a time when political and social movements have been promoting authoritarian causes on a basis of anti-intellectualism, the universities have frowned on political action by liberal student activists.[16]

[16]Harold Taylor, "The Academic Industry," in S. M. Lipset and S. S. Wolin (eds.), *The Berkeley Student Revolt: Facts and Interpretations* (New York: Doubleday & Company, Inc., 1965), p. 62.

It need hardly be said that the experiences of students in the civil rights movement, in peace activities, and in other community service programs provide rich opportunities to more broadly stimulate the cultural life of the national vocational university. In fact, creative uses of youth culture about which some writers speak so often requires institutional anchorages, especially for those students who are neither socially nor intellectually privileged. Indeed, "colleges provide at their best the closest thing we have to an initiation, one in which the cultural heritage is not so stamped onto the bodies of the young, as transmitted to their minds and senses."[17]

The gains of institutional innovation are also found in the concerns that cultural and political activities can bring to the bureaucracies of the public vocational university. A more varied and decentralized campus makes possible the wedding of youthful skills and the normal processes of institutional life. Unrestrained mass participation can breed its own anti-intellectualism in the name of "freedom" or "student's rights." But tempered by intellectual discipline and plentiful resources within the institution, a more healthy state of affairs than apathy or alienation is conceivable.

In addition, the varied life styles of the young and their experiences in community organizations, tutoring the disadvantaged, and more conventional political activity provide a rich source of experiences that shape intellectual pursuits.[18] Given the poverty of spirit and encounter that so often comprises the normal life cycle of the national vocational university, the energies of youthful encounter enrich the processes of social learning.

ENHANCING LIBERAL STUDIES

A fifth option—one usefully considered in connection with some previous proposals—is to utilize organizational structures for de-

[17]David Riesman, "The Search for Challenge," in David Riesman (ed.), *Abundance for What and Other Essays* (New York: Doubleday & Company, Inc., 1965), p. 346.

[18]For instance, Thomas J. Cottle's insightful study of personal need patterns among student activists in his "Revolt and Repair: A Comparative Study of Two University Tutorial Movements," *The Sociological Quarterly*, 8 (Winter 1967), 21–36.

veloping cultural liberalism within the national vocational university. While there are numerous types of student research projects, a university corps of research centers devoted to relevant undergraduate research would provide institutional substance to varieties of innovations in the academic culture. The root idea of the national vocational university as a social vehicle for society suggests the corresponding need for intellectual enclaves devoted to enhancing the quality of social and humanistic inquiry.

Student research centers, concentrated in the social sciences and the humanities and manned by professional staffs, would provide the opportunity for original inquiry. In addition, they would bolster large-scale opportunities for integrating affective and cognitive learning, the experiences of community participation with those of the lecture. Finally, in the maze of the national public university, such research centers would symbolically replace the liberal arts college that was once central in the scheme of the campus. Such organized centers of academic activity are potent instruments for making personally meaningful the masses of information now disseminated on the training grounds of the knowledge-based society.

Liberal studies are possible in the national vocational university only if scholarly, technical, and research apparatus are available for student use in dealing with major social and political issues. Student research centers would do away with the bifurcation between research and undergraduate education insofar as the skills and inclinations of the academic culture permit. Liberal studies can enhance social and political knowledge only if they are based on the same intellectual and methodological plane as comprise the core of the vocational university system itself.

PART II
CURRICULUM, POLITICS, AND STUDENT WELFARE

Introduction

Formal education provides one source of social and political learning in American society. Basic personality structure, family relations, and the expectations of political institutions themselves contribute to a person's acquired perspectives about the ongoing political order. Yet within the university, potentially powerful agencies are utilized or ignored, provided explicit political content or so managed as to avoid confronting linkages between personal and political orbits.

Contemporary students of education and political life are less likely than their predecessors to be impressed by the consequences of any particular formal curriculum. The abstraction and verbal symbols of the curriculum, although potentially significant, are often unrelated to the personal sources of general and political learning. The idea of the "experiential curriculum" raised in Chapter 4 draws on the vitality of instruction for human development. Moreover, the criterion of personal development provides a yardstick with which to gauge the human (and political) consequences of formal instruction in the vocational university.

The teaching of politics has always been a controversial issue in the schools. Elementary and secondary schools are sensitive to political pressures from groups within their communities. Higher learning has tended to draw a distinction between academic and political instruction as a result of discipline inclinations and the imperatives of specialization. However, teaching politics means more than indoctrination in the creeds of Marxism or the Republican party. The antipolitical rationale draws sustenance from the belief that the vocational university is apolitical in its concern with the techniques of knowledge rather than with a particular kind of political learning. Chapter 5 offers an analysis of "political teaching" as well as some alternatives geared to human needs and political awareness.

There was a time when the student culture was a matter of fun and sociability. This is no longer the case, as the account of cultural learning in Chapter 6 makes clear. Indeed, the quality of a student culture is an important element in the level of intellectuality and political learning evident on the campus. After reviewing several means by which student culture at the vocational university might be strengthened, the discussion in Chapter 6 turns to the models available for emulation at elite colleges and universities.

Chapter 4
The Experiential Curriculum

Consideration of countervailing policies designed to enhance the welfare state university leads to an analysis of curriculum. Consider at one extreme a curriculum devoted to perpetuating an explicit political ideology about government's purposes, the qualifications of rulers, and the qualities of citizenship to be rewarded.[1] Now consider scientific knowledge, unwedded to any political outcome, at the other end of the continuum. In the latter situation, the variety of courses brought to the student's attention is confined only within the prevailing state of knowledge and the diverse viewpoints in the academic disciplines. It is this latter situation that most approximates the reality within the national vocational uni-

[1] See the account of Soviet rulers' efforts to transform the educational system into the primary agency of political socialization in Jeremy R. Azrael, "Soviet Union," in James S. Coleman (ed.), *Education and Political Development* (Princeton, N.J.: Princeton University Press, 1965), pp. 233–271.

versity, with its democratic profusion of courses which range from hotel management to existential philosophy.

REDUCING POLITICAL CHAUVINISM

Academic fundamentalism comes in many forms, but the chauvinistic glorification of the national state dominates the uses to which textbooks and the educational academy are employed. In the liberal tradition, one purpose of a university is to reduce such parochialism and to expand that rare capacity for selective criticism. It is this catholicity that was a major finding in a recent study of Oxford students:

> The majority of the students regarded themselves as Europeans, and say it in so many words: "I consider myself as European"; I would like to think of myself primarily as European." One student described the prevailing attitude in the following way: "We travel in the Continent for our holidays, we wear Italian-style clothes, we read French novels, see Italian and French films, often speak one of the European languages. We consider ourselves primarily as good Europeans, so we are for Britain in Europe. Britain is inevitably mixed up with Europe."[2]

In American education, the incidence of political chauvinism has apparently declined with the expansion of professional knowledge and the influence of students and faculty.[3] Moreover, American political chauvinism (that is, references to the unique and nationalistic character of "democracy" or "good government" as an American monopoly and the glorified treatment of American politics) has increasingly withered with the strengthening of civic education and social studies programs. Chauvinism is reduced by presenting new information; hence, it is effectively countered by educational programs. For instance, the degree of overt authoritarianism can be reduced by providing distinct instruction for authoritarian students.

[2]Ferdynand Zweig, *The Student in the Age of Anxiety: A Survey of Oxford and Manchester Students* (New York: The Free Press, 1963), p. 23.
[3]Note the literature reviewed in Coleman (ed.), *Education and Political Development*, pp. 601–605.

TEACHING PARTICIPATION

Yet despite the reduction of xenophobia, there remain profound problems for the development of civic competence in the national vocational university. Concern with provincialism and intolerance was based on the antirational elements in learning processes. Bolstered in part by its minority status and sense of avant-garde élan, universities—particularly those emphasizing the social sciences and the humanities—had a primary stake in reducing intolerance and expanding the range of civic options.

The expansion of political participation comprises one critical concern in civic education. Yet available evidence illuminates the limitations of the educational system in enhancing participatory norms. The absence of social trust, learned interpersonal skills, and self-esteem retards the university's ability to foster a participatory democracy. Moreover, a certain structural congruence in the university seems to be required before participatory inclinations in its students can be stimulated. There is little evidence that the vocational university provides the supportive structure for such participatory encouragement.[4]

Clearly designed for an ascending bourgeoisie, nurtured by independent professions and laissez-faire economics, visible in the pluralism of ethnic, regional, and class schools, the liberal arts college and its rational-activist curriculum did provide a structure for teaching the role of the average citizen. The contemporary realities of the citizen role in the democratic welfare state are fairly summarized by Milbrath:

> As we think about the role of the average citizen, we should not expect him to give a lot of attention to, and be active in resolving issues of public policy. Nor should we expect him to stand up and be counted on every issue that comes along. The most we can expect is that he will participate in the choice of decision makers and that he will ask to be heard if an issue comes along that greatly concerns him or on which he can make some special contribution. Many citizens do not even vote or speak up on issues, yet their passive role

[4] See Edgar Litt, "Education and Political Enlightenment in America," *The Annals of the American Academy of Political and Social Science,* 361 (September 1965), 32–39.

has the consequence of accepting things as they are. Indeed, it is impossible to escape at least a passive role in the choice of decision makers. The choice processes can provide and government can continue to function even if many citizens choose to be so inactive as to fail to vote.[5]

The declining emphasis on participation as a function of the educational system is directly related to the assimilation of minority groups holding views inimical to the welfare of the state. The withering away of both pluralistic liberalism and the social structure supporting it suggests the anachronism of participatory civic education. The forum *par excellence* for the teaching of this national norm was the small liberal arts college with its emphasis on legalistic and humanistic studies and on the conventional learning of governmental forms and institutions.

The crucial fact about the development of American secondary and collegiate public education is the extent to which the liberal ethos of the self-cultivating, participating citizen was adapted from the private schools.[6] In the progressivism of Dewey, in the writings of George Counts, in the missionary zeal of the great schoolmen, the civic role of education was clear: to reconstruct society and to train a responsible citizenry. In operational terms, this meant that the belief system and self-concepts of the urban, immigrant masses had to be changed.

In this scheme, it could not be assumed that a liberal education subsumed socialization for voluntary participation in a pluralistic political system. Civic education became an overt, although poorly articulated, instrument of state policy. "Americanization" meant that the schools had to create a loyal and integrated citizenry. Beyond obtaining political loyalty, the schools explicitly sought to alter the normative and cognitive dimensions of politics. In essence, it was a strategy of inducements and deprivations. In order to succeed and to obtain the fruits of social mobility and political respectability through education, the immigrant had to change the nature of his political vocabulary. Thus, the signs of the good citizen became nonpartisanship instead of the urban political machine; merited public achievement instead of patronage

[5]Lester W. Milbrath, *Political Participation* (Skokie, Ill.: Rand McNally & Company, 1965), pp. 144–145.
[6]Litt, "Education and Political Enlightenment in America," pp. 32–39.

and familial loyalties; a harmony of community interests instead of the overt "selfishness" of interest-group conflicts.

The official political culture of the "melting pot" school system did appear to transmit political identification and allegiance. But, in its fundamental differences with the political institutions of ethnic groups, it failed to change the style of urban politics radically. In historical perspective, the major accomplishment of the old civic education program was to promote consensus, to use conventional information about American history and institutions to dampen "dysfunctional" radical politics.

Perhaps in their transformation of the national political ethos, the schools did not overcome the realities of emerging political forms. But they did play a role in reinforcing basic Americanism, teaching civic literacy, and fusing socialization with industrial progress. Dewey's ideas of progressive education did not liberate the child from the local restraints of the Vermont small town, but those restraints were irrelevant in the urban core. However, Dewey's ideas did help to liberate and nationalize education—"from parish to nation," in Riesman's useful phrase—and to initiate recruits into the industrial order.

It is from this liberation that a new vocabulary of civic education developed. The child is to be socialized, adjusted, and acculturated to the prevailing political order. The national welfare university is ideally suited to the performance of this explicitly apolitical function, for without a class or ideological base, intimate relations with government and the corporations perfect neutral technical competence. Indeed, a society at the height of its power and wealth can convince itself that it no longer needs civic education programs to enrich the life styles of its burgeoning collegiate population. Linked to a viable cultural base, the national vocational university becomes the perfect instrument for preserving the civic culture and, thus, for conserving the political order as the domain of specialized expertise.

Yet there remains an alternative view, in which the educator's function is to shake the acquired certainties and fear of dissent among the occupants of the national vocational university. The strategy of "unblocking" by dramatic teaching of critical social issues is of uncertain use in this context. Consider the reflective observations of a political scientist teaching in a large public university:

The university must give preference to that knowledge which is least likely to be sponsored and supported by any other institution of society, that knowledge only anxiety and fears prevent men from pursuing, that knowledge which is most needed because of these widespread apprehensions. I shall call it dissensual knowledge. . . .

The resistance of the public to the proponent of nonconventional belief is automatic. It can be active or passive, and I have seen both types among my students. Active resistance takes the form of overt rejection; the less acceptable teachings are discounted as being impractical, "long-haired," or heretical. Passive resistance takes the form of systematic, but unconscious, misunderstanding, selective perception, and gross distortion of the teacher's message. Active resistance is somewhat easier to deal with than passive, because it exists on the conscious level and is therefore a possible topic for debate. . . . In the great majority of cases, resistance is passive, i.e. inarticulate, unrealized, amorphous. Passive resistance, at the same time, is most likely to result in the severance of all possible community ties between the teacher and student; it makes communication impossible.[7]

In a complex political society, the unarticulated resentments of the citizenry may aid the demogogue's quest for a mobilized following or increase the sense of apathy with which political events are greeted. In the vocational university, so firmly committed to national politics, the accommodation to institutional demands limits the efficacy of intellectual "shock treatment."

Nor will apolitical socialization to vocationalism be eroded simply by appeals to higher scholarship or refuge in exotic styles of elite culture. Thus, in one university already committed to vocationalism, 75 percent of the freshmen class rated the practical, job-oriented task of the university as most important. By contrast, only 18 percent thought that a general concern with ideas was among the three most important functions of the university. Against this pragmatic view of education, which is reinforced by

[7]Frank Pinner, "The Crisis of the State Universities: Analysis and Remedies," in Nevitt Sanford (ed.), *The American College: A Psychological and Social Interpretation of the Higher Learning* (New York: John Wiley & Sons, Inc., 1962), p. 947.

parental attitudes, bolstered by limited peer contacts, and supported in the findings of the mass media and the social sciences that education positively correlates with earned income over a lifetime, "idealistic" appeals will probably be as ineffective as the religious appeals of a Taoist in predominantly Christian America.

What then are the curriculum's alternatives to the types of functional socialization provided by the welfare state university? Between the outmoded requirements of participatory skills and the anxiety-arousing concerns of "dissensual knowledge," a core curriculum devoted to human development provides a testable alternative. Its political consequences are to be found in the problems of racial and status policies that have long plagued democratic systems, problems to which an enlarged college-educated public ought to bring more flexible responses.

The potential role of the university in responding to human needs is influenced by internal and external factors. Thus, the formal rationality of the vocational education system provides the framework for an antidevelopmental curriculum that lacks intellectual models for the young. The practical orientation of the vocational curriculum retards that imaginative use of knowledge that potentially liberates the human personality. Effective teaching does not call a student's attention to his private motives or mechanisms; instead, it undertakes to show something of the variety and complexity of the social world of which the student is a part. Moreover, a developmental curriculum presents one's inner feelings and the diverse motives and mechanisms of other peoples. In this way, a developmental curriculum can broaden a student's self-awareness by inducing empathy with many kinds of people and by confronting him, whatever his age, with the deficiencies in his old, automatically adopted values, so that in experiencing conflicts, he is required to make new decisions. In the highly developed person there is a rich and varied impulse awareness, with many different impulses having found differentiation and integration of the ego. Such ego growth is hampered both by authoritarian or overprotective regimes as well as by permissive or chaotic ones. So, too, is impulse awareness ignored in the type of structural avoidance characterized by the vocational university's emphasis on the practical curriculum.

The internal mechanisms inhibiting the fruition of a developmental curriculum are also reinforced by social factors. A lower-middle-class college requires high intellectual eminence to compensate for the absence of many sophisticated upper-class and upper-middle-class students who have a less vocational, or immediate, definition of education's aims. Ironically, then, in the diploma-image college, where vocationalism is rampant, it is often a very low order of vocationalism and students have only the most limited sense of what opportunities might otherwise be available to them. Without an innovative academic culture, the agencies for socialization can easily degenerate into clubs or mass service stations that confirm students in their lower-middle-class outlooks and obstruct not only acquisition of a social veneer, but also any tentative efforts by the students to move toward a broader and more complex understanding associated with political-cultural elites, where technical skills count less than social and intellectual skills.

PERSONAL AND POLITICAL DEVELOPMENT

The vocational university encourages antidevelopmental tendencies in the curriculum that further repress impulse expression and complex orientations. The logic and interpersonal realities of the vocational university emphasize discipline and hard work in the extreme: an emphasis on the correct answer in a mass lecture, the expulsion of deviants, and the repression of unarticulated thoughts in the freshmen's initial pruning. Moreover, in the vocational university there is an undue abstractness and orientation to method for its own sake, a segmentation of presentation and experience that reinforces the existing value structure.

The consequences of an antidevelopmental curriculum are neither personally nor politically neutral. In Sanford's description of the college freshman, controls developed for the purpose of inhibiting impulses are still unseasoned and uncertain; in fact, they are likely to operate in a rigid manner: that is, to be rather overdone, as if the dangers of their giving away altogether were rather real.[8] Like authoritarian personalities, the strong impulses are directly opposed by an alert, rigid, and punitive conscience. The ego has to devote so much of its energy to restraining impulses that its other functions are not well performed. The extent to which vocationalism that is reinforced by an antidevelopmental curricu-

[8]Nevitt Sanford, "Developmental Status of the Entering Freshmen," in Sanford (ed.), *The American College,* pp. 253–282.

lum becomes the major socializing role of the national welfare university is a matter of personal and political concern. The latent political consequence is that more flexible and humane politics are never seen as possible and alternatives to obnoxious public policies are rejected a priori on the basis of learned suppression.

Alternatives to an antidevelopmental curriculum range from the learning of new role requirements in campus workshops to the establishment of cooperative living units. Yet the thesis that an individual's knowledge is part of his personality and, thus, to be enhanced or suppressed by the operating curriculum has been most often applied to the humanities. It is in the humanities that restrictions on imagination and creativity built up over the years can be forcefully engaged. Literature and philosophy, the arts and creative science, if not preprofessional in nature, catch the eye of the observer concerned about the developmental processes of a university education. It remains for Professor Aiken to articulate the humanistic legacy:

> The main virtue of the "tradition" for many of us has always [been] its immense virtue as a repository not just of "ideas," "ideals" and "commitments," ethical, political or otherwise, but also of artistic, literary, and religious, as well as philosophical and scientific, achievements—actualizations and consummations of the mind's powers of creation and invention—which are perennially absorbing on their own account to any teacher or student worth his salt. . . .

> The virtue of the entire tradition of liberal education has been in the liberation of the mind and soul of the student himself. . . . When all has been said our impossible task, one worthy of Virgil himself, is that when we withdraw, what will bid us farewell is not just a scholar or idea man, but the semblance of a free human being. Is this not the one commencement in which we have a deep wish to take part? And after all, is this not the true reason why we have refused to turn general and liberal education over to the secondary schools so that the institutes for advanced study can provide faster, more efficient, drier runs for future careerists and service men—men, that is to say, all too like ourselves?[9]

[9]Henry David Aiken, "The University II: What Is a Liberal Education?" *The New York Review of Books* (November 3, 1966), 24.

The uses of the humanities in impulse training and in the cultivation of intellectual and political sensitivities may abide in the humanistic tradition. Indeed, the social and natural sciences may produce comparable results. However, it would be unrealistic to place such burdens on the existing curricula and the frail shoulders of the professors who man them. To be sure, attention to a curriculum's viability is important. But these internal changes are most fruitful when there exist articulate norms of behavior, models of conduct, and a framework conducive to the analysis of social and political life.

It is precisely the absence of such a supportive culture that characterizes the vocational university as a creature of the state and, being such, designed to rationalize the training of skilled workers in a period of immense national power and responsibilities. The terms "federal-grant university" and "multiversity" are realistic descriptions of the bankruptcy of ideas and political education among those institutions most directly in view. The vocational university is a dependent entity, a creature of the instrumental needs it supposedly requires. No scientific or elite culture, no vision of social inquiry or political enlightenment makes the vocational curriculum viable. The internal development of the vocational university and its political significance may be seen in the context of the social and intellectual forces shaping it.

Each and every feature of the vocational university's existence and influence, abstracted knowledge as it is currently practiced in the antidevelopmental curriculum, represents a bureaucratic enlargement. In an attempt to standardize and rationalize each phase of social inquiry, the intellectual and interpersonal operations of the welfare state university are becoming more bureaucratic. These operations tend to make studies of man collective and systematized. There is a progression of routines, for efficiency's sake if no other, as rationalized as that of any corporation's accounting department.

In terms of "socialization," this is a perfectly sensible progression, in that the product of the vocational university is to be geared to the "accounting department" of the nation. The political uses of vocationalism, in turn, have much to do with the selection and the shaping of new qualities of mind among the personnel of the school, qualities both intellectual and political. As it is practiced in the vocational university, abstract knowledge and the antidevelopmental curriculum have come to serve whatever ends its bureaucratic clients have in view. Those who promote and practice this style of training readily assume the political perspectives of their bureaucratic clients and chieftains. To assume the perspective is often, in due course, to accept it. Insofar as such training efforts are effective in their declared practical aims, they serve to increase the efficiency and the reputation—and to that extent, the prevalence—of bureaucratic forms of domination in modern society. But whether or not effective in these explicit aims, they do serve to spread the ethos of bureaucracy into other spheres to cultural, moral, and intellectual life.

The external features shaping the welfare state, or public vocational university's curriculum are to be found in selective attention to political inquiry. Unlike the land-grant college's relation to a local elite, the vocational university's primary funders are federal agencies, and the subtle muting of alternative inquiries and life styles is rooted in this relationship. While the quality liberal arts colleges and the eminent research universities have a wealth of professional power upon which to draw, the public vocational university exists in a more insecure environment. Hence, the efforts at bureaucratic rationalization inhibit the critical consideration of social and political policies promulgated by governmental sources of largess.

The consequence of formal rationality becomes the effective isolation of students from their efforts to comprehend social reality and its relation to them. By depending upon a necessarily bureaucratic kind of training, a taboo in the name of science and administrative practicality is placed upon student efforts to become independent and substantive thinkers. Vocational training encourages men to fix their social beliefs by reference to the authority of an alien apparatus, and it is in line with and reinforced by the bureaucratization of reason in our time. The industrialization of academic life, in particular the fragmentation of problems of social inquiry, cannot result in a liberating educational role for initiates, nor can it sustain such a role for engaged social scientists.

The vocational university's antidevelopmental curriculum creates a fragmented milieu in contradistinction to the job of liberal education and the political role of the social sciences and the humanities and their intellectual promise, which is to enable students to transcend such fragmented and abstracted milieux and to become aware of historical structures and the place of the individual within them.

The critical curriculum reform within the vocational university is less to be found in classic literature of social science methodology than in core studies that are devoted to the function of the vocational university and the role of social inquiry and action within it. This return seems consistent with the evolution of a number of currently flourishing academic enterprises, such as social welfare and the behavioral sciences themselves. Once confined to the practical and usually low-status position of community agencies, such enterprises fought their way to academic respectability and power. Developing professional ties and research skills, they formed important alliances with powerful established interests in the federal government and the private economy. Indeed, the newly formed vocational universities are partly the legacies of these trends. In many cases, the youthful passion and inquiry of practitioners in the vocational university has subsided in favor of the premature rationalization that impedes the cultural and political sensitivity of a current student generation.

Educational inquiry into the mission and organization of the vocational university itself becomes the critical curriculum innovation. It is through inquiry that social scientists and other educators can make their educational institutions a liberated framework in which publics can exist, at least in the beginning, and one in which discussion is encouraged and sustained. A core curriculum revision becomes a matter of adequately defining the vocational university's public role in relevant terms. The educational and political role of the vocational university's core curriculum should be to provide and act upon the self-knowledge that helps to cultivate and sustain publics and individuals so that they can develop, live with, and act upon adequate definitions of personal and social reality.

In earlier periods of academic life, such introspection served the needs of pedagogues and the institutional apparatus that was usually located in schools of education. The current rationale of the vocational university is to sever the study of politics and education from any direct bearing on the development of persons and agencies servicing human needs. Christian Bay's critique of the transformation in the study of politics has strong application to the vocational university's antidevelopmental curriculum:

Perspectives on the aims of politics or philosophy or social analysis become transformed from a focus on systems maintenance. . . . There has subsequently been no significant attempt [to find] a better approach to the study of human needs, so that it can be determined how good or bad particular institutions and policies are for human beings.[10]

It is only in a core curriculum that is devoted to the fruition of human intellectual and personality needs that the major structural reformation of the vocational university is to be found. Such a curriculum would examine the relation of the university structure to the centers of corporate and governmental power influencing it. It would, as the center of an ongoing course of study, provide legitimation to the unexpressed needs for enhanced self-esteem and cultural realization currently inhibited by the functionalism of the vocational university. Moreover, it would fuse the present bifurcation of cognition and impulse reinforced in the vocational university's segregation of personal concern and formal requirements. Such a curriculum would also lead to the cultivation of imagination and alternative possibilities within the vocational university and the political systems creating it. Concerned about the political and personal confusion implanted within the vocational university's average initiate, the core curriculum's examination of the educational structure's affect on social and intellectual well-being provide a community of interests that would enable the isolated student to develop his potentiality.

To be sure, there are other roads to the cultivation of civic knowledge. A culture-bearing class, such as that located in elite universities, has already socialized the relations between personal and political behavior. A subculture, rooted in ethnic or regional norms, may be reinforced or explicitly challenged by the academic mandate of the vocational university. However, it is the supposed neutral character of the vocational university and its latent function in suppressing personal impulses with social consequences that makes the incorporation of a revised core curriculum that is devoted to the educational and political role of the vocational university so useful—and necessary.

[10]Christian Bay, "Politics and Pseudopolitics," *American Political Science Review,* 59 (1955), p. 44–45.

The social and academic incentives of the vocational university strongly encourage the diminution of social inquiry.[11] By linking the vocational university to its political meaning in society, a revised core curriculum would incorporate intellectual incentives; that is, the satisfaction the student perceives in the striving to broaden his understanding and sharpen his powers of perception. In the vocational university, such incentives have been marginal, perpetuated, if at all, by "radical" student groups and a few professors. The organizational response to intellectual incentives is enhanced if they become part of the ongoing academic structure, ideally the core program among undergraduates. For it is only such relocations of institutional power that are viable within the context of the functional welfare university.

Curriculum innovation is itself a major means of providing intellectual and emotional support to undirected inquiry, of breaking down the barriers to participation and political learning created in the one-dimensional structure of the vocational university. Every social order seeks to mold and train its young to celebrate the past and the present, not to educate them to think freely and responsibly about political ideals for the future. The vocational university is a suitable instrument for such efforts to create pliant citizens. Its efforts are usually met with compliance, although at times with rejection, thus perpetuating the pseudoeducation of current generations.

Such compliance is not likely to be changed by angry mass movements or by traditional student radicalism. It is more likely to be changed by incorporating inquiry about the university within the mainstream of the educational endeavor. Thus, structural change becomes the prerequisite to behavioral and political change. For only then can the more anxiety-provoking subjects of political conflict and loyalty be rationally discussed. Only then, when self-esteem and intelligent participation are valued by the institutional structure, can the political dilemmas in the knowledge-based society become matters of concern beyond the self-perpetuating nationalism of the vocational university.

[11] I have drawn on the excellent ideas of Christian Bay in his "A Social Theory of Higher Education," in Sanford, *The American College*, pp. 972–1006.

Chapter 5
The Teaching
of Politics

The formal organization or structure of the vocational university effectively blocks substantive inquiry about political issues from the masses of its students. Its organization makes it convenient for the vocational university to ignore the importance of substantive issues. Moreover, in no way is the organization or structure of the vocational university related in any constructive sense to the life choices of its students. Thus, personal avoidance is matched by institutional screening in that the question about the teaching of politics in the vocational university is somewhat beside the point. But in fact, "politics" *is* being taught, to the extent that prevailing power ratios within the university or between powerful and deprived groups are unquestioned. Moreover, in the metaphysics of institutional accommodation to the requirements of American foreign and domestic policy, such political apologetics as support of Vietnam policy are cogently impressed upon young minds who are the first in their families to attend college.

THE CHANGING RELATION OF POLITICS
TO EDUCATION

The political relationship between teaching and the vocational university corresponds to the changing patterns between educational and political orders. For much of American history, the universities were the stage on which accommodations among competing groups were resolved. In the conflicts between church denominations, between fundamental Protestantism and the more generous boundaries of urban modernity, the ethos of the university was involved. Herein developed the norms of academic freedom and the rights and duties of professional responsibility in fulfilling one's obligations to the scholarly community, the students, and the diverse publics beyond the university. In fact, the major impact of American universities was to liberate educated men from the confines of local prejudice and mass opinion. It was this conservative function, vividly acted out in the McCarthy period, that bolstered the currency of scholarly inquiry and more effectively paved the way for broader institutional accommodations.[1]

These accommodations have proceeded apace since the end of World War II. Scientists, administrators, and more recently social scientists have established firm relations with their counterparts in government and research. The older "liberal ethos," often most vigorously defended by social scientists, has become part of the national ethos in that knowledge is now broadly valued. Herein the issues of political learning assume an importance unanticipated by earlier polemics. For instance, the concern of educators with the civic capacities of their students was supported by a liberal ethos and the role of "culture bearer" as an attribute of the teaching profession. The newer roles of researcher and administrator are accompanied by a diminution of the older concern and sense of minority solidarity that propelled the assault on popular ignorance and its supporters in the corporate structure.

While other governments have rendered the educator politically neutral or ineffective, the successful American strategy is to assimilate him to new professional models. Thus, in the context of the vocational university, debates about the scientific study of politics without political involvement sound archaic. Moreover, professional norms support a separation of political concerns as

[1]Paul F. Lazarsfeld and W. Thielens, Jr., *The Academic Mind* (New York: The Free Press, 1958).

citizen and professional concerns as scientists, thus reducing tensions between academics and their publics. It is in this sense that the credo of an end-to-ideology politics within American politics (and concomitantly between American intellectuals and large-scale political concerns) has its greatest meaning.[2] Such politics as remain are in the confines of professional lobbying and in the performance of scholarly work on behalf of numerous private and governmental agencies. The assimilation of the political intellectual, then, in the sense to which intellect bears some independent and critical relation to public policies, marks an important clue to the probable consequences of political instruction in the universities. Hereafter, such instruction would more carefully follow the fault lines of discipline specialization, the requirement of no personal commitment to a particular research outcome's having political consequences and the emphasis upon methodological sophistication in the conduct of inquiry.

An additional consequence is in the trading of publics. While an essentially bourgeois academic culture found dialogue between adults and students useful, the new relations between government agencies and professional-training establishments render the old relationships less meaningful. The result is that social inquiry becomes detached from concerns with older publics (intellectuals, minority groups, political reformers) and more concerned about political relations with men of power. Indeed, perspectives about the powerful become more refined and more muted in the proliferation of client relationships. The educational academy is becoming more like older professions, such as law and medicine, and hence more removed from emotional and reform involvement in public affairs.[3]

[2]See Daniel Bell, *The End of Ideology* (New York: The Free Press, 1962); the debate between Daniel Bell and Henry David Aiken in *Commentary* (April and October 1964); and Seymour M. Lipset, *The First New Nation* (New York: Basic Books, Inc., 1963), esp. pp. 213–224. These three selections are reprinted in Edgar Litt, *The Political Imagination: Dialogues in Politics and Political Behavior* (Glenview, Ill.: Scott, Foresman and Company, 1966). Empirical evidence associating the increased social status of American intellectuals with their political conservatism is reviewed by Lipset in his *Political Man: The Social Bases of Politics* (New York: Doubleday & Company, Inc., 1963), pp. 332–371.
[3]See Kasper D. Naegle, "Clergymen, Teachers, and Psychiatrists: A Study in Roles and Socialization," *Canadian Journal of Economics,* 22 (February 1956), 46–62.

This development has increased the social and political vacuum within the vocational university and among the citizenry with which it must deal. Aware of social inquiry's complexities from professional experience and methodological training, the professional does not expect to devote his major efforts to the personal development of the untutored. Nor is he likely to use the raw material of student concerns with political issues as the basis for an education in a liberating sense. No longer an intellectual provincial or deprived individual, the professional would regard prescriptions such as this pointless:

> What I am suggesting is that by addressing ourselves to issues and to troubles, and formulating them as problems of social science, we stand the best chance, I believe the only chance, to make reason democratically relevant to human affairs in a free society, and so realize the classic values that underlie the promise of our studies.[4]

Thus, viable student cultures dealing with academic and intellectual matters are unsupported by the structure and organization of the university. After all, the movements for peace, civil rights, and educational reform in American universities have been essentially student-led movements that are uncongenial to the professional uses of social knowledge.[5] At the same time, more grave issues of national policy, especially in the areas of national security and foreign policy, have been items on which academic perspectives are influenced by the need for new and powerful clients. The prudent caution about the explicit teaching of political values and beliefs within the vocational university seems a distorted view.

The average student in the vocational university is highly dependent upon the agencies of information and opinion formation that are used to justify existing policies. Thus, the transformation of knowledge so that it lacks personal or political referents becomes "dysfunctional" for the student in clarifying choices and assessing such evidence as does exist about substantive matters.

---

[4]C. Wright Mills, *The Sociological Imagination* (New York: Oxford University Press, 1959), p. 194.
[5]The combination of organizational, career, and psychological pressures constricting open-ended articulation of political issues is investigated by Harmon Zeigler, *The Political World of the High School Teacher* (Englewood Cliffs, N.J.: Prentice-Hall, Inc., 1966).

Moreover, such reification supports the functional imperatives of the vocational university and its reluctance to bear directly on the major social and political issues of the day.

Without previous cultural exposure, the products of the vocational university are particularly amenable to symbolic manipulations and unconsidered appraisal of political events. It is this displacement of intellect that is the critical force in the perpetuation of the antidevelopmental curriculum in the vocational university. The displacement of intellect and the established role of the scholar-expert in the welfare state importantly condition the absence of issues, much less alternatives, that purport to enhance the political responsibility of the welfare state university's graduates. Thus, the most enduring role that can be performed within the vocational university should be to cultivate that flexible commitment of the loyal opposition, to show that men may analyze and disagree with major governmental policies without dethroning "authority" or being untrue to their professional capacities. Realistic instruction in a mature polity is to be found in the effort to unblock educational capacity in the developmental curriculum.

The developmental curriculum, then, presents a critical perspective with which to enhance the student's cognitive functions and emotional supports in dealing with social inquiry. The historical progress of the knowledge-based society and of men of knowledge within it has not existed long enough to provide a complete analysis. Yet several points are clear. First, the expansion in social knowledge and techniques has not been applied in politically neutral ways. Social theories have become a matter of major national policy in issues ranging from urban development to the dimensions of foreign policy. Beneath the "liberal consensus," a variety of intellectual concepts have had political consequences. The theory of games is as applicable to American policy in Southeast Asia as it is to small-group research. Systems analysis is a fashionable tool that can be used in numerous types of social engineering. So, too, can intellectual matters be symbolic devices for diverting attention from certain political realities:

A good case can be made for the conclusion that there is indeed something of a consensus among intellectuals who have already achieved power and affluence, of those who sense that they are "being honored" in this society. It is also true that this consensus is most noticeable among the scholar-

> experts who are replacing the free-floating intellectuals of the past. In the university, these scholar-experts construct a "value-free technology" for the solution of technical problems that arise in contemporary society, taking a "responsible stance" towards these problems. . . . This consensus among the responsible scholar-experts is the domestic dialogue to that proposed, internationally, by those who justify the application of American power in Asia, whatever the human cost, on the grounds that it is necessary to contain the expansion of China.[6]

Second, the assimilation of academics and the emphasis on technical proficiency has muted a concern with the substantive analysis of public policies. Teachers require social, professional, and psychological supports in order to feel comfortable about the selective uses of their critical appraisals. It is often easier to relegate substantive problems to other "political" agencies and strive for innovation only on the methodological and conceptual levels. These latter nuances are lost in the transmission of new findings to the practitioners within the vocational university. It is this neorealism that is most convincingly learned in the vocational university.

Lacking both the elementary tools of critical appraisal as well as intellectual self-confidence, the student in the vocational university may come to feel that the problems of justice, world peace, and domestic policies are unworthy of reflection because so little effort is made to incorporate them in developmental teaching models. It is no wonder that the student responds to such abstracted knowledge in an uncomprehending way or, in rare cases, reaches conclusions such as these:

> The central task of political science as a profession is to extol the present order, criticize other existing systems, and debunk radical and utopian political thought. In America in the 1960s, the task is to praise democracy, identify this particular concept with the existing social order by way of praising also pluralism and "free enterprise" in the same breadth, and to condemn communism; in fact, all ideologies are suspect, and the end-of-ideology literature seeks to conjure them

[6]Noam Chomsky, "The Responsibility of Intellectuals," *The New York Review of Books* (February 23, 1967), 23.

away. Of basic importance is the modern redefinition of "politics." No longer does the term refer to the promotion of justice or the search for the best organization of social life.[7]

Nor is extensive political content now being offered that will yield more informed judgments about the social worlds perplexing thoughtful men. The norms of apolitical teaching are to be found in the peculiar convergence of modern professional knowledge and the vocational university.

Thus, studies about the effectiveness of alternative teaching methods, for instance lecture versus discussion, are likely to conclude that "objective information" is more effectively transmitted by the lecture method—the imagined advantages of face-to-face contact do not come forth in experimental situations. Of course, what is lacking in such efforts is any attempt to indicate how effectively the teacher's efforts to unblock constricted impulses comes across to the students.[8] Nor has there been a follow-up to see in what ways students internalize knowledge and change their behavior in intergroup relations, discussion of foreign policy, and programs of urban planning.

The students in the vocational universities are overwhelmingly white and from the lower-middle or working class; they view the university as a means to vocational opportunity. Their response to abstracted empiricism and the avoidance of sensitive issues about race relation or American policies in Vietnam is patently a case of reinforced socialization. The application of useful techniques to practical tasks is perfectly consistent with some increased support of "tolerance" or "internationalism" at the general level these notions are tested in survey instruments.[9] Yet teacher avoid-

[7]Christian Bay, "The Cheerful Science of Dismal Politics," in Theodore Roszak (ed.), *The Dissenting Academy* (New York: Pantheon Books, Inc., 1968), p. 36.

[8]An analysis of teaching methods in political science is provided by William S. Livingston's "The Challenge of Numbers," and Robert H. Connery's "Now Bring Together," in R. H. Connery (ed.), *Teaching Political Science* (Durham, N.C.: Duke University Press, 1965), pp. 120–148 and 238–267 respectively.

[9]The relationship between cultural and international libertarianism and contextual educational processes remains uncertain, as does the relationship between learned "liberalism" and its political consequences. An example is found in the respected study by the late V. O. Key, Jr., *Public Opinion and American Democracy* (New York: Alfred A. Knopf, 1961), chaps. 7 and 13.

ance and objective testing effectively segment attitudes from probable behavior. One need not in an interpersonal way confront the objects of such behavior. Solely as a device for translating professional research findings, exceedingly abstract teaching reinforces vocationalism.

What teaching pattern has some chance of effectively stimulating responses and engaging dormant values? The answer lies in a concerted effort to engage personal values by linking them to intellectual concepts. In other words, the object of superior teaching in the vocational university is to make intellect relevant by showing its application to those situations that are important influences on the life styles and political attitudes of the average student. Here the linkage between political theory and "actor-in-situation" learning are a fruitful option to the normal processes of the vocational university.

HUMAN NEEDS AND POLITICAL LEARNING

The guiding orientation to the university is a view of political education as a devotion to the enhancement of basic human needs. A number of scholars have attempted to formulate need hierarchies and methods for testing them. In major criticisms of this attempt, notions of need progression are regarded as romantic and beyond the reasonable expectations of scientific knowledge. In this latter view, need enhancement is equated with the performance of "good works" in the province of theology.[10] Heinz Eulau provides a representative summary of such a viewpoint:

> Even if the technical problems of deriving values from human needs could be solved, there is at present little agreement among behavioral scientists about just what human needs are "fundamental," and there is a great deal of disagreement about the priority of particular needs—a priority

[10]Compare Christian Bay's two works ("Politics and Pseudopolitics," *American Political Science Review,* 59 [1965], 39–51 and "The Problem of Evaluating Political Institutions and Human Needs," paper presented at the Conference on Values and Political Science, Northwestern University, Evanston, Ill., 1967) with James Davies, *Human Nature in Politics: The Dynamics of Political Behavior* (New York: John Wiley & Sons, Inc., 1963), esp. chaps. 1–3.

that is likely to change from time to time. The difficulty is, of course, that any ordering of needs is impossible without some prior preference ordering of values.

By way of medical analogy, diagnosis (of which behavioral science is quite capable) is one thing, but therapy is quite another. Even if there were consensus on the nature of "social diseases" . . . . there is unlikely to be similar agreement on the steps that should be taken to remedy or prevent these diseases, or on the order in which these steps might be taken. The notion that behavioral science can provide the criteria for a program of social and political therapy is utopian.[11]

Nevertheless, the engagement of human values, such as self-actualization, to extant politics does provide an antidote to the blandness of the welfare university. Realistic appraisals of one's milieu and life chances are strongly rooted in experiences with important political issues. Attitudes about open housing, racial violence, and community cooperation are based on the pragmatic testing of problematic situations. Such an effort is not presently found in the political socialization of the vocational university. Unguided by parental norms, accepting on face value the university's apolitical texture, the uncritical responses to governmental authorities and public policies are products of the vocational university's graduate.

Therefore, the intellectual teaching problem in the vocational university is to implant the idea of human need enhancement as a goal of both political studies as well as general education. The impact of this course does not merely apply to the vacuum of political and intellectual criteria within the vocational university. It applies with equal force to abstracted and dehumanized outcomes in the existing pattern. The human-needs approach is designed to engage the personal attention of the learner.

THE USES OF POLITICAL CONTENT

How then might such intellectual insights be applied to enhance political teaching in the vocational university? First, it would seek

[11]Heinz Eulau, *Political Behavior in America* (New York: Random House, Inc., 1966), pp. 12–13.

to reduce the structural dissonance between latent human needs and political problems within the local community. Tutorial and community-action programs have increasingly become a normal and effective part of the life education among socially and intellectually gifted young adults in our best colleges and universities. Such initiation cannot be exorcised—and it is seldom evident— among hard-pressed young people in vocational universities. Effective teaching, augmented by a viable curriculum, would serve to put people in touch with those having ideas and values significantly different from their own. Dialogues between corresponding groups that are not within the college population, such as racial minorities and individuals with other policy positions, are supplementary devices. At the present time, the boundaries of the vocational university serve to constrict such contacts and to reinforce the homogeneity of opinion. The variety of interpersonal relations developed among the communities of scholarly, political, and social discourse counters ethnocentrism and uncritical acceptance of political issues.

The first task of an effective teacher is to support ways by which the neophyte citizen can come in contact with others. One example is in interracial contact, but less obvious are the critical discussions with authority figures, the analysis of pertinent social data, and discussions with policy experts, such as those in the fields of urban renewal and public welfare. The expansion of the cognitive and emotional fields beyond the vocational university's parameters provides the basic requirements for the degree of self-knowledge and social awareness necessary to promote the fruitful analysis of political issues. Such an expansive experiential base also provides the basis for feedback in gauging the criteria of political justice and for assessing institutional arrangements designed to maximize human potential and reduce human suffering. For instance, the projection of authoritarian impulses in unqualified support of an aggressive foreign war is a subject of experiential inquiry. So, too, can social and defensive uses of opinion formation become the focus of a liberating developmental teaching program. A rich use of community resources would include not only cultivating sensibility as a sort of therapy (in the ancient sense of clarifying one's knowledge of one's self), but also imparting all those skills of controversy with oneself, which we call thinking, and with others, which we call debate.

The creative use of teaching resources in the vocational university should also include the differentiation of roles and values that support self-cultivation and open inquiry as a way of life. The intellectual and cultural experiences of the vocational university stereotype experiences and segment periods of learning and reflection in order to further segment individuals in the service of a smoothly functioning mass society.[12] The humanization and enrichment of experiences counters this tendency and enlarges a person's capacities to comprehend and tolerate not only more information, but also information from diverse sources.

As the first business of governmental and political life, a concept of human need fulfillment is reinforced by enriching experiences among a variety of "significant others" this notion runs counter to the idea of political neutralism in the scheme of the vocational university. So, too, meaningful teaching should encourage the formation of alternative hypotheses and more subtle analyses of political events. The teaching of values, particularly the rich values of a knowledge-based society, requires the awareness of political information from unofficial sources and divergent ideological perspectives; it requires participants who can communicate their own experiences. It is not merely the stereotyped experiences that challenge the exercise of political intelligence and imagination within the vocational university. It is also the undemocratic distribution of visible sources of "public opinion" should the teacher, as molder of political cultivation and sensibility, acquiesce to the dominance of existing authoritative sources:

> Most governments would rather have their citizens concerned with anything else, even greed or corruption, rather than with rational thought. For fully rational thought or dialogue invariably raises radical questions about how to justify existing privileges and ways of oppression. To every regime, bread and circuses are preferable; or in our time mass media that entertain and indoctrinate rather than instruct. The late Henry Luce and a living dinosaur like David Lawrence with their *Time* and *U.S. News* are among the

[12]Aside from its impact on party identification, the political significance of the family seems weak among the current youth generation. See M. Kent Jennings and Richard G. Niemi, "Family Structure and the Transmission of Political Values," paper presented at the 1966 Annual Meetings of the American Political Science Association, New York City, September 6–10, 1966.

most effective suppliers of this essential service in America today, the envy of their countless competitors. . . .

Moreover, it sounds attractively liberal to argue that university teachers should instruct their students with factual knowledge but let them form their own values,—until one reflects that *Time* or the Pentagon will take over the latter part of their education where we have defaulted.[13]

The role of the teacher in articulating such political values and opinions does not stand as an isolated act, much less as a personal forum for the expression of latent emotions. Political education in the vocational university is part of a more generous effort to construct a cultural apparatus that unites personal, public, and experiential domains of knowledge. On a personal level, the cultivation of sensibilities and awareness of impulses behind public opinion is the educational prerequisite to unlocking perceptions of more distant and complex subjects. On an experiential basis, the encounters with "significant others" in the community, especially with those students and faculty for whom attitudes are rationally used, serves to make vivid the intellectual efforts of writers and artists contributing to our awareness of the human situation.

On a public level, the critical analysis of all available research and observation dealing with public policy considerations should be pursued in depth. Critical reflection on the policies and consequences of the vocational university itself provides a civic theater in the round, as it were, for cultivating discriminatory powers. And, of course, such efforts must also include an analysis of conceptual coinage supporting the proclamation and defense of established public policies. To do otherwise is to support a sense of institutional fatalism about education's efficacy in reducing irrational politics. The extent to which political irrationality does exist "ought not to justify the intellectual leap from the fact of prevailing psuedo-political behavior in our competitive, unjust, anxiety-ridden social order to the enormous assumption that . . . we are doomed to a *permanent* eclipse of genuine politics in the modern democratic world, and that no educational liberation from *Time, U.S. News,* and their intellectual equivalents is ever to reach more than a small minority of our electorate."[14]

[13]Bay, "The Cheerful Science of Dismal Politics," pp. 16, 17.
[14]Bay, "The Cheerful Science of Dismal Politics," p. 15.

Chapter 6
Student Culture in the Vocational University

Concern about the structure of the public vocational university and the political consequences of its curriculum leads inevitably to an examination of the influence of the prevailing student culture on human development. During a bucolic period of collegiate life, Woodrow Wilson observed that "you will see the true life of a college where youth get together and let themselves go upon their favorite themes—in the effect that their studies have upon them when no compulsion of any kind is on them, and they are not thinking to be called to a reckoning of what they know."[1] Such an idealistic view does not account for the pull of diverse forces currently segmenting the student culture within the vocational university. The influences on student culture in the vocational university is

[1]Woodrow Wilson, "The Spirit of Learning" (1909), in *Selected Literary and Political Papers and Addresses of Woodrow Wilson,* vol. I (New York: Grosset & Dunlap, Inc., 1925), p. 252.

the primary concern of this chapter. Its second concern will be to find a currently available model by which the civic quality of the large university's student culture may be enriched.

PEER-GROUP INFLUENCE

Such a complex social organization as the vocational university has many potential sources that can shape the dominant interests of its student body. The direction of informal group interests, rooted in face-to-face interaction among peers, is an important potential influence. Interpersonal influence is highly effective, especially when students explicitly trust and rely on the judgments of their peers. However, the potential quality of peer influences is shaped by several factors. First, the student culture may carry the cultural and political views of a specific class. Thus, at universities in which intellectual quality and political activism are highly valued, working-class students, who are not usually libertarian about civil liberties, quickly learn these dominant norms and become more libertarian than blue-collar students at other institutions.[2] Furthermore, lower-status students also absorb norms encouraging active political participation to the extent that they are members of friendship groups containing a "mix" of individuals with diverse class origins and social interests.[3] The transmission of dominant norms in the student culture among peer groups increases the effectiveness of interpersonal relations as carriers of intellectual and political traditions.

At other times, the student culture resembles a collection of small peer minorities, each engaged in unique pursuits that add to the variety of social and intellectual stimulants on the campus. However, the criteria of student selection limit the influence that peer interaction can produce. Because the vocational university

[2] See Hanan C. Selvin and Warren O. Hagstrom, "Determinants of Support for Civil Liberties," *British Journal of Sociology,* 11 (March 1960), 51–73; the middle-class cultural adaptation of working- and lower-middle-class students at such elite colleges as Antioch, Reed, and Swarthmore is also reported in Burton R. Clark and Martin Trow, "Determinants of College Student Subcultures," 1963 manuscript, p. 73. A revised version was published in T. Newcomb and E. Wilson (eds.) *College Peer Groups* (Chicago: Aldine Publishing Company, 1967).

[3] See Kenneth Langston, "Peers, School, and Political Socialization," *British Journal of Socialization,* 17 (December 1966), 419–429.

draws heavily from the lower-middle class and working class, the availability of opportunities to students to exchange diverse political views and to be exposed to new opinions is particularly critical. Usually, the student most in need of identity exploration and exposure to new views is most inhibited by the structural restraints on creative peer exchange. There is evidence that peer groups are important elements in socialization to political orientations and interpersonal skills encouraging effective evaluation of complex politics in a modern society. However, the compartmentalization of diverse social interests from intellectual and political learning is substantial. Particularly within the large, vocation-oriented university, the potentialities of peer learning are under heavy strain:

> As student bodies have become larger and less homogeneous in most American colleges, there has correspondingly arisen what might be referred to as a kind of academic anonymity. Most students develop friendships with others whom they know as persons but not as students (in the literal sense). If peer groups of importance to the members include individuals who are sharing the excitement of academic-intellectual discovery, it is almost a matter of chance. It has become less and less probable, during recent decades, that individual students who know each other well, and who are important to each other outside the classroom, experience shared excitement in the same classroom. With exceptions, which, though not rare, are far too infrequent, the domain of peer-group influence overlaps but little with the intellectual domain.[4]

The absence of pervasive peer-group influence devoted to political and intellectual interests in the public vocational university produces a vacuum that is often filled by a second determinant of student culture; namely, those interests and activities sponsored by the university itself. Students at universities stressing vocationalism are particularly adversely affected by the dearth of an informal, student-directed culture. The working, commuting student in a state college has little time for and interest in campus

[4]Theodore Newcomb, "Student Peer-Group Influence," in Nevitt Sanford (ed.), *The American College: A Psychological and Social Interpretation of the Higher Learning* (New York: John Wiley & Sons, Inc., 1962), pp. 483–484.

matters, social or political, especially if he is supporting a family. He is particularly aloof from those activities officially provided by the student government and other entertainment in the older collegiate image of "fun and games." This marginal participation is encouraged because overall important matters tend to remain with such distant authorities as the state board of education or with the upper echelon of the university's administrative staff. In a vocational university, there is little incentive for the administration to give broad powers to a student government, much less to encourage a broad array of participating student groups. Particularly among middle- and lower-status students, the result of this lack is to foreclose major means of identification with the college. The vocational university reinforces those authority systems that encourage dependency on the student culture and its peer relationships. The size and scale of the vocational university increase the need for a viable student culture, on one hand, and yet, on the other, to operate in such a way as to segregate student interests from the ongoing operation. Unless other countervailing forces exist, student culture within the vocational university reinforces divisions between social-class skills, between pragmatic and intellectual motivations, and between adolescent pseudopolitics on the campus and the broad range of worldly concerns about peace and war, race relations, and the quality of urban life that impinge on the life situations of the coming generation.

ADULT MODELS

The vigorous political and intellectual interests of the faculty provide a countervailing force to the normal dearth of an effective student culture in the vocational university. Although the segmented model of the vocational university dilutes these interests, the work and life styles of the faculty are sometimes usefully available. In particular, professional initiation and apprenticeships in research are influential in broadening the orbits of tolerance and interest among the student body. At every university characterized by vocationalism and compartmentalization, there are a few genuine cultural models, men of professional integrity and personal compassion. However, professional compartmentalization is the norm of the vocational university more fully than at elite universities, which combine specialization with broad intellectual concerns, and certainly more fully than at the liberal arts colleges devoted to undergraduate education. Moreover, it is not an inevitable result that faculty concerns, even when communicated, will transmit new ideas about intellectual and political life. The engagement of faculty concerns to the capacities and life styles of students is always a difficult task. The potential effectiveness of faculty involvement is eroded by the absence of efforts to counter the structured political and intellectual impersonality of the vocational university. Thus, at one typical large state university, most faculty members thought of themselves as political "independents" who discussed politics infrequently themselves, were fairly inactive in political campaigns, and thought that overt politics and learning did not mix on the campus.[5]

Under these conditions, social and political learning in the student culture becomes more subject to the transient concerns of overtly political speakers and the activities of ideological minorities on the campus. Without effective political evaluation by genuine academics, student culture also becomes more bureaucratized. Professional specialists in guidance, counseling, and "student affairs" become the most frequently available adult models. There is functional learning in such collegiate organization and bureaucratization because the vocational university's graduate is socialized to the realities of adult organizational life and its pervasive separation of private and public interests. However, at a time when youth is most open to intellectual and interpersonal challenge, the structure of university vocationalism is least responsive to articulated human needs. This loss is particularly important because students in the vocational university are not necessarily the most gifted and resourceful.

The quality of peer interests and its vertical linkage with the university and its professionals comprise major influences on the student culture. Yet these influences are not pervasive and, amidst the scale and impersonality of vocationalism, increase the influence of the mass "youth culture" on student life. The content of the youth culture varies from the statistically rare presence of a cohesive ideological commitment to the more diffuse influence of

[5]A. S. Edelstein, "Since Bennington: Evidence of Change in Student Political Behavior," *Public Opinion Quarterly*, 26 (Winter 1962), 564–577; the subtle communication of faculty about social and political attitudes is explored in Joseph Adelson, "The Teacher as a Model," in Newcomb (ed.), *The American College*, pp. 396–417.

mass culture on the work and play styles of young adults. The influence of monotic or noncumulative mass influences is particularly strong in light of the consequences of segmented vocationalism. Mass youth culture replaces the transitory experiences by which the young can usefully experiment not only with the adult culture in its historic context but also with diverse forms of interpersonal expression and intellectual exploration. The emphasis on mass youth culture produces a pseudoadaptive solution for the personal and social problems of young adulthood. It is a solution marked by cognitive stereotypy, value stasis, and interpersonal conformity. It is a solution that is accompanied by resistance to conflict, to change, and to the transformation of the self. It is a solution which settles for a modest resynthesis of earlier learning that closely follows the lines of the older organization of drives and defenses.

Moreover, student concerns with artistic expression and the plight of disadvantaged groups are not pervasive, thus removing major learning of adult social and political roles. The structure and authority systems of the vocational university place added stress on the problematic situation of the young making more burdensome the tolerance of ambiguity that always accompanies meaningful initiation into the ongoing social order:

> Owing to the long preparation and the relative segregation of the children's world from that of the adult, the main values of the society are necessarily presented to the child and the adolescent in a highly selective way, with a strong idealistic emphasis. . . . This [produced ambivalence] is manifest, on the one hand, in a striving to communicate with the adult world and receive its recognition; on the other hand, it appears in certain dispositions to accentuate the differences between them and the adults and to oppose the various roles allocated to them by adults. While they orient themselves to full participation in the adult world and its values, they usually attempt also to communicate with this world in a distinct, special way.[6]

The blockage of these exploratory efforts in the unprepared culture of the vocational university does not normally lead to

[6]S. N. Eisenstadt, "Archetypal Patterns of Youth," *Daedalus*, 17 (Winter 1962), 39.

compensatory political radicalism. It may result in individual social problems, but most often it fulfills society's requirements for
normal, adaptive behavior that is based on the performance of
specific technical tasks. The student culture of the vocational university is a technical training laboratory that performs the functions of the larger system.

THE USES OF STUDENT CULTURE

The lack of a student culture is most greatly felt in the social
preparation of society's "middle mass," for the failure to use student culture in cultural and political development has consequences
in the quality of formal learning. For instance, the absence of
intellectual self-confidence, skills in social inquiry, and parental
(or cultural) supports for intellectual activities produce a preference for passive lecture situations rather than dialectic seminars.[7]
The failure of the student culture to provide fertile soil in which
new relationships and roles can be tested encourages the perpetuation of mass adolescent norms. These one-dimensional standards
of evaluation and self-appraisal reinforce the absence of attention
to human development in the formal structure of the vocational
university.

The problem of the informal youth culture in the public vocational university then is how it can be more fruitfully enriched
in order to help the vocational university itself become a source
of human development. In the context of the vocational university, the task is to make student culture more available for meeting
the intellectual and personal needs of the students. This requires
a view of student culture as neither absorbed by nor alienated
from the formal university structure. It also requires consideration
of how the cultivation of public sensitivity can be internalized in
the student culture, given the absence of existing supports.

No single solution can enrich student culture in its long-
term, and probably inevitable, link with the norms of the vocational university. However, it is useful to consider "elite" student
protest movements in order to provide a model for the less differentiated culture at the vocational university. Moreover, elite

---

[7]See Joseph Katz, "Personality and Interpersonal Relations in the College
Classroom," in Sanford, *The American College*, pp. 365–395; Thomas E.
Drabek, "Student Preferences in Professor-Student Classroom Relations,"
Sociological Inquiry, 5 (Winter 1966), 87–97.

student bodies provide available persons to whom vocationally directed students can turn in search of cultural innovation and organizational cues.

AVAILABLE "ELITE" MODELS

A politically oriented student culture may provide the functional equivalent of those social and intellectual supports weakly based in the vocational university itself. The evidence of the potency of these rehearsals for political and intellectual life in a modern society has heretofore been located among youth elites. This viable student culture is strengthened by two recent developments in American society; namely, the unprecedented opportunity for participation available to advantaged youth and the assimilation of other articulate and idealistic groups in the political system. The type of student culture that provides a yardstick against which other student cultures may be judged is marked by precocious awareness of these developments. It is also complemented by early acquisition of those organizational and verbal skills prerequisite to political and intellectual life. The utility of a participatory student culture in an affluent society also includes rehearsals for professional careers in the same way that past youth movements have contributed to the skills of contemporary social scientists.

Deprivations in status, psychic well-being, and economic sustenance have often been found to be fruitful stimulants to "radical" student behavior and ideology.[8] But current evidence more clearly sustains alternative interpretations that are useful in evaluating mass student cultures in American universities. Recent student protest movements have not been randomly distributed among American universities. The three campuses on which there have been the most student demonstrations (the University of California in Berkeley, the University of Michigan in Ann Arbor, and the University of Wisconsin in Madison) are among the nation's leading universities and probably the three most eminent state institutions in terms of national rank of scholarly achievement.[9] More-

[8]This is a constant theme in the work of S. M. Lipset; see his "University Student Politics," in S. M. Lipset and S. S. Wolin (eds.), *The Berkeley Student Revolt: Facts and Interpretations* (New York: Doubleday & Company, Inc., 1965), pp. 1–9; see also his "University Students and Politics in Underdeveloped Countries," *Minerva,* 3 (Autumn 1964), 13–56.

[9]Seymour M. Lipset, "Student Opposition in the United States," *Government and Opposition,* 1 (1966), p. 1–35.

over, R. E. Peterson reports that, among 849 American colleges and universities, "institutional quality defined by the proportion of faculty doctorates, was moderately correlated with protests over off-campus issues and negligibly, though positively, correlated with protests regarding internal issues."[10] While there is no hard evidence on the contribution of specific university populations to the peace and civil rights movements, veteran activists maintain that the Ivy League, quality, private liberal arts colleges (Amherst, Antioch, and Reed, to name only three) and state universities in the progressive tradition (for example, California, Wisconsin, and Michigan) have made disproportionately high student contributions to the peace, poverty, and civil rights campaigns. The contribution to university educational reform is less certain, although here too there is evidence that large elite universities have undertaken educational experiments and programs whose fruition was doubtful without recent student efforts and direction.

There is considerable evidence about the social characteristics of student activists at some of these elite universities that suggests guidelines for creating a viable student culture amidst vocational dominance and collective impersonality. At the University of Chicago, in May 1966, protests against the military draft were led by students who perceived themselves to be upper-middle class and who tended to come from high-income families and from families where the father is likely to be a highly educated professional.[11] At the University of California in Berkeley, students with high academic achievement and liberal political attitudes comprised the core of the Free Speech movement.[12] Heist found that the Berkeley Free Speech Movement drew extraordi-

[10]R. E. Peterson, *The Scope of Organized Student Protest* (Princeton, N.J.: Educational Testing Service, 1966), p. 46.

[11]Richard Flacks, "The Liberated Generation: An Exploration of the Roots of Student Protest," Working Paper No. 1 (Chicago, Ill., August 1966 [mimeo]).

[12]Cf. Paul Heist, "Intellect and Commitment: The Faces of Discontent," Western Interstate Commission for Higher Education and the Center for the Study of Higher Education (Berkeley, Calif., 1965 [mimeo]); Selvin and Hagstrom, "Determinents of Support for Civil Liberties"; Robert Somers, "The Mainsprings of the Rebellion: A Survey of Berkeley Students in November, 1964," in Lipset and Wolin (eds.), *The Berkeley Student Revolts,"* pp. 530–557; William A. Watts and David N. E. Whittaker, "Some Socio-Psychological Differences Between Highly-Committed Members of the Free Speech Movement and the Student Population at Berkeley," *Journal of Applied Behavioral Science,* 2 (Winter 1965), 21–42.

nary large proportions of students with intellectual orientations. Moreover, on measures of social alienation, social introversion, impulse expression, and anxiety, Heist also found that FSM participants scored about the same as did comparable groups in the student population on measures of social integration. Christian Bay, in a secondary analysis of Berkeley data, argues persuasively that the radicals were personally highly integrated individuals.[13]

A closer look at the leadership core during the FSM led Heist to conclude that a composite of characteristics differentiated nine of the eleven core leaders from the general student population. These extraordinary young people were differentiated by their high level of cultural sophistication, degree of sensitivity, and awareness, by the extent of their libertarian orientation, the intensity or level of their intellectual disposition, and the state of their readiness to be involved or active in behavior beyond campus norms. At Chicago, Flacks was impressed by the divergence from conventional life choices among the high participants. Whereas seventy percent of the nonparticipants in the draft sit-in selected "career" as one of the three most important life areas, only about one-fourth of the student activists concurred. Rather, the "world of ideas" and "working for national and international betterment" turned up as the leading life goals of the activistic students.

While students who actively create and use a campus culture are probably more varied than these studies suggest, a realistic composite picture of participatory student culture is discernible. At high-quality colleges and universities, a student subculture composed of highly intellectualistic, humanitarian, personally resourceful and, at times, romantic individuals provides the viable element in the student culture. Moreover, this subculture provided the basis for constructive criticism of the university and other social institutions. As products of economic affluence, sensitive to experience and avoiding raw moralism, usually themselves sons and daughters of cultivated parents, activists in the contemporary cultural student movement are not products of disadvantaged circumstances. The high-quality student culture attracts the most advantaged and often the brightest sector of the student body. Indeed, the social and intellectual characteristics of these students are often the results of parental permissiveness and equalitarian-

---

[13]Christian Bay, "Political and Apolitical Students: Facts in Search of Theory," unpublished manuscript, 1967.

ism within the home. In references to standards of the liberal, cultivated individual, the participating students and their cultural creativity are the benefactors of the equalitarian and participatory family advocated by Dewey and Freud.[14]

The themes of protest and the criticism of conventional career patterns in American society by this cultural force are also significant. A quest for self-expression conveys a rejection of conventional restraints; antiauthoritarianism is equated with a strong antipathy to arbitrary rule; equalitarianism connotes a belief in a wide dispersion of social and political power; antidogmatism resists the appeal of doctrinaire or ideological interpretations of events; and an emphasis on community encourages the expression and awareness of impulses. Moreover, there is a frequent counterposing of bureaucratic norms to communal norms, a testing of the former against the latter.

To be sure, the degree of youth's expressive solidarity in these themes impresses the psychologically attuned eye. But it would be a mistake to dismiss these protests of our most intelligent and sensitive youth as being merely social-psychological in character. On the contrary, the student protest movement among these advantaged youth at our best universities points to several cultural strains in American life. One revealed strain is the gap between the functional and personal meaning of education, the view of training perfected in the vocational university and the liberal cultivation of intellect and sensitivity supported by other collegiate models rooted in history.

Within reasonable proportions, the elements of the American student movement just described draws on upper-status young adults to perform the functional equivalent of an older radical tradition that was usually located in an ascending social class and certain ethnic groups.[15] That earlier tradition sought to break the bonds of ascriptive and parochial values within American society. The narrowness of the small town and the exclusion of minority

[14]The evidence of Richard Flacks at Chicago and most of the Berkeley studies suggest the need to reconsider the proposition that parental discord accompanies student political radicalism. Evidence supporting that proposition is examined in Robert E. Lane and David Sears, *Public Opinion* (Englewood Cliffs, N.J.: Prentice-Hall, Inc., 1964), pp. 17–33.
[15]An excellent discussion of political intellectuals in several historical periods is found in Lewis Coser, *Men of Ideas: A Sociologist's View* (New York: The Free Press, 1965), esp. chaps. 19–21.

groups animated a ferment of political ideas and literary expression. The contemporary cultural uses of the university are found among the legatees of modernity, precocious cosmopolites whose sensitivity to politics and ideas begins in childhood. The triad of student culture, its relation to the university, and social criticism in America is not a new one. Indeed, the most compelling analogue to the role of student culture at high-quality universities is that of "unattached intellectuals" in European and American society. Unattached intellectuals are those individuals who value ideas more than institutional attachments and who, as a consequence, have often occupied marginal positions of power and status within their societies. In America, political and literary radicals have been effectively absorbed within dominant political and academic institutions. Universal skill attributes rather than ideological or political styles are the criteria for recruitment in complex organizations. The coterie and the salon are swallowed up in the organizational pyramids of the mass media and the publishing industries. It is difficult to find American colleges of any quality whose curriculum is distinct from the contents and expectations of national professional societies and academic disciplines. Moreover, the ideology of radical protest and modernization are intellectual curiosity pieces now sentimentalized in the nostalgia of middle-aged reflection. In effect, the absorption of American radicalism and its political and literary men has been a major factor in recent cultural history, with important consequences for the American political culture.

While earlier radical generations used minor political parties, Bohemia, and literary magazines as focal points from which to criticize American institutions, contemporary student activists are themselves firmly within the major institutional bastions of the society, indeed within the most distinguished universities and colleges themselves. What has happened is that part of a generation liberated from the anxieties of privation and discrimination has demanded that universities deal anew with root social and political problems of our society. This view and the behavior accompanying it may be either praised as intellectual fortitude or branded as intellectual irresponsibility. The more critical point is that the fruits of early socialization are being realized within an institutional setting, namely, that of select American universities. In an oblique way, an earlier emphasis on character training ("personality development" in modern usage) within American colleges in the era of denominational zeal has been revived on the initiative of secular students. Here the extension of participatory skills to include broader segments of the population and the elite corps of American youth is evident as a normal part of the educational process. Where earlier participatory norms were acted out in the mass political party and the voluntary association, the energy that used to go into college play is displaced into serious political and intellectual concerns that include the quality of the university itself.

The quality of student culture in the vocational university might be enhanced by provision of more resources to support latent student intellectual and political capabilities. As noted earlier, adult models in institutional, administrative, and faculty are inadequate for this task. More promising is a selective use of the youth culture developed at quality universities that is adapted to the ideas and programs of the vocational university. This modification of a type of cross-cultural peer learning provides a major source of innovation to the often lackluster tone of the vocational university's student culture. Furthermore, the use of elite youth leaders provides that degree of informality essential to the basic trust required in a genuine academic culture. In this union of affective and cognitive learning lies a viable base for student culture and human development.

A viable student culture provides the environment for a sequential learning that links the social perspectives of youth to those of adulthood. The impetus for change within the vocational university's student culture must be of sufficient strength to make a difference and of such integrity that it will be seen in positive terms by vocationally oriented students. The local sources of peer learning are too weak and lack alternative models to vocationalism on which the vocational student can draw. Institutional innovation either neglects the student culture or renders it more fragmented in the interest of physical and administrative expansion. The available mass youth culture lacks the qualities of cultural play and expanded political perspectives to promote new learning.

Cultural development in the vocational university will take place—if it takes place at all—at a time when higher education itself is generally rooted in established and conservative human practices. The vocational universities are sluggish and marginal in intellectual quality and in their utility for human development; technologically and administratively they are quite dynamic and firmly established in the mainstream of bureaucratic institutions. Although some sense of marginality is likely to impel change, the social and intellectual position of existing student culture is too weak to encourage ideological movements or the formation of a counterculture directed at the centers of vocationalism itself. Nor does the distribution of intellectual quality and political self-esteem in the vocational university make these promising courses of development for the students themselves to pursue. Student culture in the vocational university is particularly in need of innovative supports rather than hostile efforts directed against the entire existing system.

In this context, the most promising sources of student cultural development are interclass and interinstitutional models. These models for constructive cultural change are available at any number of elite universities and colleges. They are found in the personal and social quality animating fruitful change in the quality of university student culture at these most dynamic institutions. An accelerated exchange of students and research professionals among universities of differing cultural quality would at least provide the glimmer of alternatives to the vocational university. In addition, such exchange would provide the cultural base that could be institutionalized by later developments. The rudiments of a cultural base could be used to integrate social and academic matters for students on a comprehensive campus.[16] This reform blends into the articulation of alternative models of student culture which is present in patterns of participation among elite youth but which is not found to any degree in the architectural revisions on the large, vocation-directed campus.

[16]The articulation of student motives with campus esthetics is discussed in Clark and Trow, "Determinants of College Student Subcultures."

PART III
HUMAN DEVELOPMENT AND POLITICAL LEARNING

Introduction

The preceding analysis of the relationship between politics and the public vocational university calls attention to the relationship between education and human development, for another reason to investigate politics and education is reflected in the theories of "political socialization." Political socialization is the process by which individuals within a political system learn the norms of that system in order to enable it to function more effectively. This central theme of individual adaptation to an existing political system complements the vocational and bureaucratic drift of university processes previously investigated in this book. The first chapter of this part contains a synthesis of the evidence concerning the political impact of formal education. Although this chapter concludes that the specific educational factors influencing political attitudes are uncertain, important political qualities, such as liberalism and political information, are cumulatively influenced in the educational system. As Chapter 7 indicates, this liberating syndrome of education, anchored in the tradition of rational political education, is not sustained by the functional socialization to skills and tasks dominant in the public vocational university.

Since most socialization studies are concerned with the political attitudes supporting the abstract political system, there have been few inquiries into the impact that personal values have on the educational system as a political culture. In discussing this aspect of political learning in terms of the high school, Chapter 8 indicates how the school's authority structure as well as its curriculum are politicized by the actors involved in them. The values of both the school administrators and the students are revealed as critical factors in the quality of political response that is forthcoming during the college years.

Educational systems need not be mere conduits through which politically socialized graduates are transported. On the contrary, the rapport between personal values and educational systems complements the larger political significance of the new welfare universities. That larger political significance is explicitly assessed in Chapter 9, which relates the problem of political dissent and obligation to the contours of knowledge shaped in the public vocational university.

Chapter 7
Education and Political Socialization

Why succession mean ed this institutional death

No political system would support educational institutions that deliberately produced graduates who had learned to distrust ongoing politics or to plot revolutions against the present order. However, without some proscriptive guidelines, the consequences of education for political life remain obscure. Although that theme runs throughout this book, this chapter attempts to clarify some extant knowledge about the political socializing effects of education.

INFLUENCE OF THE AUTHORITY STRUCTURE

Two dimensions of importance are the mechanisms by which political education occurs and the particular consequences of these efforts. The schools have been found to influence political learning through a variety of mechanisms. However, it is difficult to isolate the specific influence of such factors as the school's authority system, its curriculum, and its social climate. Considerable attention has been devoted to the study of early childhood socialization. Those who have focused upon this stage of political learning argue that the most crucial and lasting political orientations are formed in childhood. These orientations are crucial because they influence the development of subsequent political attitudes and because they are freely and uncritically adopted.[1] According to this view, in order to understand adult political attitudes, it is necessary to study the development of the largely informal, affective attachments of early childhood. This suggests that the influence of elementary school may be the most crucial educational experience in terms of influencing political attitudes. However, those who have studied childhood socialization have often failed to isolate the specific effects of school attendance. They have naturally concentrated on describing the orientations of young children without isolating the effects of the various socializing agencies. As a result, we cannot uncritically accept the view that the elementary school is more crucial in terms of socialization than high school until the effects of other socializing agencies are held constant.[2] It is not sufficient to simply point to the comparatively large degree of attitude formation during the elementary school years.[3] On the other hand, there is substantial evidence that orientations developed toward the political regime are formed early in childhood.[4] These political orientations appear to be learned through an informal process in which the child's relations with his immediate authority are extended to remote authorities. The family situation, often the child's relations with his father, is a crucial determinant of the child's image about political authority.

However, authority relations outside the family are also prob-

[1]See Fred I. Greenstein, *Children and Politics* (New Haven, Conn.: Yale University Press, 1965), pp. 121–135; David Easton and Jack Dennis, "The Child's Image of Government," *The Annals of the American Academy of Political and Social Science*, 361 (September 1965), 40–57.

[2]Robert Hess and David Easton, "The Role of the Elementary School in Political Socialization," *The School Review*, 70 (Winter 1962), 257–265.

[3]Greenstein, *Children and Politics*, pp. 120–121.

[4]David Easton and Robert D. Hess, "Youth and the Political System," in S. M. Lipset and Leo Lowenthal (eds.), *Culture and Social Character: The Work of David Riesman Reviewed* (New York: The Free Press, 1961), pp. 226–251.

ably influential. Hence, the elementary school would be expected to play a crucial role in the development of the child's attitude toward the political regime. In fact, the school's influence is largely an indirect learning process in which affective orientations arise through contact with the authority structure of the school and classroom. In addition to the importance of the authority structure of the elementary school, there is evidence that the curriculum influences the cognitive orientations of young children.[5] In the areas in which the school is likely to be important in teaching political attitudes, differences in attitudes between lower- and upper-status children disappear, providing more grounds for believing that education can play an important role in cognition about politics in which lower-status children are deficient.

In general, although a significant amount of political learning occurs during the childhood years, it is not clear that the school broadly contributes to these influences. The necessity to focus more closely on the political influence of specific agencies of socialization, such as the elementary school, is clear.

By the time that the child enters high school, the most crucial orientations toward the political regime have been formed.[6] Much of this socializing influence occurs through a nonexplicit learning process. This leads us to think of the elementary school experience as rather distinct from high school and university experiences. In the latter, only minor changes in broad orientations toward the regime and the political system would be expected. Socialization at the later educational stages centers about participation and the acquisition of specific attitudes toward civil liberties and government economic policies. Moreover, this later learning occurs through more conscious processes.

While a qualitative distinction between elementary education and later school experience is warranted, such a distinction is only partly appropriate in considering the political influences of high school and college. The effects of the curriculum and social climate do appear to be continuous between the two levels of education. Similarly, the political orientations produced by these factors are also probably reinforcing. While the student's attitude

---

[5]Greenstein, *Children and Politics,* pp. 55–84.
[6]Robert Hess and David Easton, "The Role of the Elementary School in Political Socialization, pp. 261–263.

toward participation may be more susceptible to influence in high school than in college, attitudes toward civil liberties and socioeconomic matters are developed throughout the educational experience.

However, the influence of the school's authority structure appears to be much more pervasive in high school than in college. While a number of efforts have been made to describe this structure and its effects, by far the most intriguing account is presented by Edgar Friedenberg.[7] Friedenberg presented students with a hypothetical situation and offered a variety of possible responses to this situation. The students were then asked to rate the responses. These ratings provided considerable insight into the social and political nature of the high school students. The sample of students studied was not random nor statistically significant, but students did vary according to the socioeconomic character of the student body and public versus private endowment of the institution. Briefly, Friedenberg's thesis is that the average high school contains a highly authoritarian and manipulative authority relationship which inculcates authoritarianism and undemocratic attitudes, if not deeper personality taints, within its students. Rules are rigid; students are treated as objects, not as individuals, and the administration is alienated from its clientele; creativity is discouraged; students are not granted responsibility; and initiative is feared.

Friedenberg's conclusions are supported by other scholars. An equally undesirable social climate in the schools is fostered to complement the authority structure. Hence, students come to treat one another in a fashion similar to that in which they are treated by the administration.[8] The consequences of the system are not hard to imagine. The concepts of dignity and privacy are not permitted to develop; power comes to be respected regardless of the way in which it is used; legitimacy and due process are not regarded as important. The values that are adopted are superficial and other-directed. It is always the individual that is wrong, never the system.[9]

---

[7]Edgar Friedenberg, *Coming of Age in America* (New York: Alfred A. Knopf, 1965) and "The Modern High School: A Profile," *Commentary,* 45 (November 1963), 77–79.

[8]G. D. Spindler, *Education and Culture: Anthropological Approaches* (New York: Holt, Rinehart and Winston, Inc., 1963).

[9]Jean Grambs, *Schools, Scholars and Society* (Englewood Cliffs, N.J.: Prentice-Hall, Inc., 1965).

INFLUENCE OF THE SCHOOL CLIMATE

It is one thing to locate the sources of political repression in the school's authority system; it is something else to relate it to the social climate of the school. The fact that the social climate of a school may have an important socializing effect has been recognized by many researchers. Most have failed, however, to appreciate the difficulties in assessing this factor. The very notion of a social climate is a rather vague concept. It is applicable to any number of levels, ranging from the family to the nation. On these higher levels, the notion of attitude climate is often used as a catchall explanation for differential shifts in partisanship which cannot be explained on the basis of immediate environment.[10] The difficulties in measuring attitude climate on these broader levels are very great; on the more restrained plane of an educational institution, they are still difficult and require careful consideration. It is important to note that the attitude climate may have little to do with the curriculum that is taught or even with the attitudes of the instructors. The staff may be isolated and able to make little impact on the dominant norms contained within student social structures. The question then becomes whose attitudes are to be measured in determining what is the dominant climate of opinion? For instance, efforts to ascertain the partisan climate of student opinion simply by counting student heads—by finding the proportion of students from Republican backgrounds as compared with students from Democratic backgrounds—seems unsatisfactory in that it weighs all students equally. This method does not take account of the political views among the teaching staff.

The problem of attitude weighting in socialization also applies to the effect of social-class dominance on political opinions. A number of studies indicate that in heterogeneous peer groups within American schools, lower-status students tend to shift their attitudes in the direction of those held by upper-status students.[11] This pattern is not limited to American society. In a study of Jamaican high schools, Kenneth Langton found that children from the lower socioeconomic class were more likely to have assimilated participant norms when they attended socially heterogeneous

[10]See Martin Levin, "Social Climate and Political Socialization," *Public Opinion Quarterly,* 25 (Spring 1961), 596–608.
[11]See Levin, "Social Climate and Political Socialization," p. 599.

schools. The impact of participatory norms was even greater when the lower-status children were members of a socially heterogeneous friendship circle.[12]

However, a number of studies by James Coleman indicate that high social status may not be the key factor in measuring peer influence within a given high school. In a study of a number of Midwestern high schools, Coleman found that those students who were outstanding athletes and those who were most socially popular were acknowledged by their peers as the dominant social leaders.[13] The results of Coleman's study indicate that this type of student leadership acts to reduce interests in public concerns, such as politics, and to emphasize social skills and the more frivolous pursuits of youth. In fact, Jennings and Niemi, in a highly provocative article, note a weakening of partisan feeling among high school students as compared with their parents, though this may have been caused by other factors.[14]

Katz and Lazarsfeld have demonstrated that it is probably a mistake to see opinion leadership as some diffuse attribute.[15] They suggest, rather, that there might be specialists in each interest area. The problem is how to identify and isolate these specialists, in view of the fact that reference and peer groups may exist for various members of any community, and thus many different attitude climates may exist simultaneously in one social setting. Thus, both Goldsen *et al.* and Selvin and Hagstrom find that fraternity men are exposed to a different attitude climate than are nonfraternity members of the college community.[16]

One further component of the attitude climate at colleges and perhaps even at high schools is the expectation of future up-

---

[12]Kenneth Langton, "Peer Group and School and the Political Socialization Process," *British Journal of Sociology,* forthcoming.

[13]James S. Coleman, "The Adolescent Subculture and Academic Achievement," *American Sociological Review,* 65 (Fall 1964), 337–347.

[14]M. Kent Jennings and Richard Niemi, "Family Structure and the Transmission of Political Values," paper presented at the 1966 Annual Meetings of the American Political Science Association, New York City, September 6–10, 1966.

[15]Elihu Katz and Paul F. Lazarsfeld, *Personal Influence* (New York: The Free Press, 1955).

[16]Rose Goldsen *et al., What College Students Think* (Princeton, N.J.: D. Van Nostrand, Inc., 1960); Hanan C. Selvin and Warren O. Hagstrom, "Determinants of Support for Civil Liberties," *British Journal of Sociology,* 11 (March 1960), 51–73.

ward social mobility. Dodge and Uyeki in a study of engineering students note that those students from Democratic families who were most conscious of their impending rise in status were the most likely to shift their partisanship in the Republican direction.[17]

INFLUENCE OF CURRICULUM

Having analyzed the impact of authority structure and the school's social climate, the discussion now turns to a consideration of the curriculum's impact on political attitudes. Some studies find that course content does matter; other studies find that it is of little political significance.

First, both the content and expectations of the civic education curriculum are best understood when the specific historic period of a nation's political development is taken into consideration.[18] Thus, efforts to absorb large numbers of immigrants into American civic life enhanced the extent of direct efforts to improve civic education in a very personal way. More recently, attention to the rational performance of the American system, supported in the main by a highly integrated and allegiant citizenry, has shifted from humanistic and politically selfconscious learning to technical and apolitical vocationalism. The discussion of the vocational university in this book represents an awareness of that development.

Even when direct efforts are made to influence political learning through the curriculum, the results are likely to vary with respect to the political content that is being influenced. First, the content of civic education programs is likely to be influenced by community expectations, which differ among socioeconomic groups.[19] Lower-middle and working-class students are likely to have a more idealistic and passive view of politics taught to them stressing political harmony. On the other hand, upper-middle-class students were oriented toward a "realistic" and active (participa-

[17]R. W. Dodge and E. S. Uyeki, "Political Affiliation and Imagery across Two Related Generations," *Midwest Journal of Political Science,* 6 (August 1962), 216–226.

[18]This argument is developed more fully in Edgar Litt, "Education and Political Enlightenment in America," *The Annals of the American Academy of Political and Social Science,* 361 (September 1965), 32–39.

[19]Note Edgar Litt, "Civic Education, Community Norms, and Political Indoctrination," *American Sociological Review,* 28 (Fall 1963), 69–75.

tory) view of politics stressing political conflict and bargaining. However, more short-term attitudes, such as those supporting democratic processes and nonchauvinistic sentiments, are subject to considerable influence by an imaginative civic curriculum.

The limitations of the curriculum in altering views about long-term citizen participation and a rational-activist stance toward the political world are confirmed by other studies. One important research asked whether increased information about politics results in a greater motivation to participate in public life and whether the degree of political interest is at all related to the extent of student mastery of political course material.[20] Data was gathered from two types of introductory courses—an integrated course in the social sciences and a more traditional course in American government. In addition, two sections of the integrated social science course were taught: one indirectly encouraged greater political participation, while the other heavily and directly stressed the relevance of participation for young citizens. The findings were disappointing: None of the courses succeeded in affecting students' attitudes toward participation, and the two hypotheses mentioned above were not substantiated by the data.

However, there is evidence that civic courses may crystallize uncertain beliefs about the efficacy of political participation. Although the curriculum did not affect the direction of student opinion, Ray Horton's nationwide study of high school youth supports this more modest, but important, reinforcement function of civic education in the schools.[21]

The studies mentioned above all deal with courses focusing directly on government and politics. Many of these political courses have an explicit message in regard to personal beliefs about politics, especially the efficacy of the rational, active citizen. If the influence these courses have on political attitudes is debatable, then it would be surprising if the nonpolitical curriculum had a profound socializing influence. However, here there is conflicting evidence about the curriculum's political influence. On the one hand, there is the inventory presented by Jacob, who concludes that the

[20]Albert Somit *et al.,* "The Effect of the Introductory Political Science Course on Student Attitudes toward Political Participation," *American Political Science Review,* 52 (December 1958), 1129–1132.
[21]Ray Horton, "American Freedom and the Values of Youth," in H. H. Remmers, (ed.), *Anti-Democratic Attitudes in American Schools* (Evanston, Ill.: Northwestern University Press, 1963), pp. 110–134.

curriculum has no effect upon student attitudes, any changes that occur are the result of the school's social climate which may or may not have a profound influence on the political beliefs of the student.[22] On the other hand, Alex Edelstein summarizes a large number of studies that find that students in the humanities and the social sciences are more liberal than students in business administration, engineering, and the natural sciences.[23] However, neither Jacob nor Edelstein report on the extent that intervening factors were held constant in the various studies they summarized, and it may be wondered whether self-selection, rather than course influences, does not often underlie the liberalism of social science and humanities students. A reasonable conclusion is that the curriculum has a modest influence on student attitudes when they are positively supported by the more pervasive social climate of the campus.

The discussion thus far has focused on studies that are concerned primarily with specific socializing factors, such as the curriculum, contained in the educational process. Some of the problems encountered in discerning the particular influence of these specific processes have been discussed. This chapter now turns to a consideration of attempts to study the total consequences of the education experience.

CUMULATIVE EDUCATIONAL INFLUENCES

The traditional focus of education's cumulative impact has been upon the possible liberalizing effects of education. However, "liberalism" is a somewhat vague term, and it has been used differently by various writers. Jacob, for instance, uses liberalism to connote a capacity for critical independence in the utilization of personal resources that deal with political and social issues. This definition seems to combine inexactitude, on the one hand, with overrestrictiveness on the other. Hence, it seems more useful to consider liberalism in two separate, but related, areas; namely, attitudes toward civil liberties and civil rights and attitudes toward federal economic welfare measures.

[22]Paul E. Jacob, *Changing Values in College* (New York: Harper & Row, Publishers, 1957).
[23]Alex S. Edelstein, "Since Bennington: Evidence of Change in Student Political Behavior," *Public Opinion Quarterly,* 26 (Winter 1962), 564–577.

Based on knowledge of support for civil liberties and democratic norms among the adult population, it would be expected that education would have a liberalizing effect. Indeed, considerable consensus is found that supports the proposition that education enhances civil liberties in most of the important studies. Education encourages support of civil libertarianism, and this outcome is true on the high school as well as on the college level. Ray Horton, for example, while generally noting that a significant percentage of high school students do not support civil liberties (no attempt is made to compare them with the adult population), finds that higher grade levels are positively correlated with increasing support for civil liberties.[24] However, no attempt was made to investigate college dropouts, so that it is possible that what is being presented here is a weeding out of more illiberal students from lower socioeconomic backgrounds rather than a change in attitudes toward civil liberties. It also ought to be noted that opposition to principles of "Marxist ideology" and feelings of anti-communism, although not increased nationalism, also increased with academic grade performance. An earlier study by Remmers and Radler also located a positive correlation between education and support for civil liberties, although this relationship was less significant than Horton reports.[25] In addition, a study by Mainer conducted over a five-month period indicates that (racially) intergroup programs explicitly introduced in the high school curriculum have a significant effect in bolstering tolerance, although, like so many of the conclusions presented in this area, there is no clear indication that the new learning will continue into later life.[26]

Turning to studies of higher education, Selvin and Hagstrom found in a 1957 study at the Berkeley campus that support for civil liberties increased consistently at each school class level.[27] Such critics as Jacob contend that these findings do not indicate a real tolerance of diversity, but rather that education has merely

[24]Horton, "American Freedom and the Values of Youth," pp. 115–118.
[25]H. H. Remmers and D. Radler, "The Citizen He Will Become," in H. H. Remmers (ed.), *The American Teenager* (Indianapolis: The Bobbs-Merrill Company, Inc., 1957), pp. 41–72.
[26]Robert Mainer, "Attitude Change in Intergroup Education Programs," in Remmers, (ed.), *Anti-Democratic Attitudes in American Schools*, pp. 122–154.
[27]Hagstrom and Selvin, "Determinants of Support for Civil Liberties," pp. 62–65.

succeeded a culturally supported social norm that is useful in getting along with others. This criticism is questionable because increased support of civil liberties is based upon a distinct interpersonal sociability characteristic of American youth. Education's influence on the tolerance of groups and people difficult to "get along with" bolsters the frail sociability acquired during the adolescent years. It seems to be an independent and important contribution of quality education at elite colleges and universities.

Although the precise contribution of course content to the support of civil liberties is debatable, Edelstein found that at the University of Washington students in general educational programs were more likely to become civil libertarians than those students in technical and vocational areas.[28] It may be argued that this is more a matter of self-selection than the effect of the curriculum itself, with the more civil libertarian students gravitating toward the liberal arts and the conservatives toward the vocational schools. However, an attempt was made to meet this objection in a study of citizenship attitudes of graduating seniors at Purdue in 1949.[29] The study compared graduates in the material sciences, who had some general education courses, with engineering students who did not have general education courses. Moreover, an effort was made to control other factors by holding constant the family backgrounds of the students. In fact, both exposure to general and special education produced increased support of civil liberties. The influence of the university and its curriculum may be very limited and of little consequence in stimulating more active political participation among students. But at the college level, at least, greater support of civil liberties is an important consequence of a liberal educational experience. It is in this experience of enlarging the orbits of tolerance, to which universities have a long-standing commitment, that the role of the social sciences and humanities curricula are critical.

In regard to economic welfare liberalism, the conclusions are much less definite, more subject to the play of specific policy issues and the particular time and place at which the studies were carried out. Although it is not surprising that the highly educated in general should have conservative economic attitudes (since

[28]Edelstein, "Since Bennington," pp.
[29]A. J. Drucker and H. H. Remmers, "Citizenship Attitudes of Graduate Seniors at Purdue," *Journal of Educational Psychology*, 42 (Spring 1951), 231–235.

college students come from higher socioeconomic groups), the question remains as to the impact of the educational process on social welfare values.

The results of Newcomb's Bennington study are well known, although the increase in economic liberalism during the New Deal undoubtedly remains a special case in a special time.[30] However, it is interesting to note that some earlier studies of the effects of college in the 1920s showed pronounced shifts in the opposite direction; namely, the college experience increased the economic conservatism of its graduates.

More recent studies show little agreement about the collegiate impact upon socioeconomic attitudes. Edelstein finds that the tendency of students at the University of Washington to change their economic attitudes in a liberal direction is twice as frequent as the reverse, while Middleton and Putney in a study of sixteen colleges found that those students whose attitudes had shifted away from that of their parents were considerably more likely to have moved in a more liberal than conservative direction about economic policies.[31] Selvin and Hagstrom found a similar shift, supporting a broad federal role in economic amelioration at Berkeley and refer to it as a "declassing" consequence of education. The norms of the humanitarian welfare state are firmly based in collegiate experiences.

On the other hand, the study by Rose Goldsen et al. on the Cornell campus, begun in 1952, shows students becoming more economically conservative after college, but this tendency is small.[32] Moreover, in a broader ten-campus survey, socioeconomic backgrounds were found to be unimportant in predicting the economic attitudes of the students, which points to the strong, liberal, socializing effect of the colleges. However, a number of significant criticisms have been directed at this research. Only the Cornell study measured change over time; much of the data is likely to have reflected the national political climate, the questionnaire was

[30]Theodore M. Newcomb, *Personality and Social Change: Attitude Formation in a Student Community* (New York: Holt, Rinehart and Winston, Inc., 1943).

[31]R. Middleton and S. Putney, "Political Expression of Adolescent Rebellion," *American Journal of Sociology*, 48 (March 1963), 527–535.

[32]Compare Selvin and Hagstrom, "Determinants of Support for Civil Liberties," with Goldsen *et al.*, *What College Students Think*, pp. 51–65.

poorly constructed; finally, obvious faults were present in the methodology.[33]

Another study of 661 Southern California college students found that while seniors were significantly more liberal than freshmen on a variety of civil rights and socioeconomic questions, these differences were basically attributable to academic selection rather than to educational processes.[34] Differences between the upper- and lower-class students became negligible once sex and grade-point averages were held constant. However, McClintock and Turner neglect the possibility that differences in mean grade-point averages between the classes may be due as much to a general upward shift in the averages of all students over time as to the dropping out of the poorer students.

Jacob also concludes that college has little liberalizing effect, at least in areas of economic policy attitudes. However, it should be noted that among others, the conclusion of this inventory is based on the Goldsen study mentioned above. Yet the breadth of the material that this inventory covers does give it a certain authoritativeness which cannot be ignored. The Jacob study, however, has been criticized on a number of methodological and conceptual grounds.[35] It is interesting to note that even Jacob, who is usually pessimistic about education's political impact, notes that certain schools with self-conscious philosophies or purposes and with close and informal student-teacher relations can have profound effects in changing student's political values and attitudes.

The political impact of education is limited by prevailing forces in the American political culture, the general apolitical social patterns of the American youth culture, and competing interests that diffuse interests within the university framework itself. Yet the quest for long-term liberalizing effects of a college educa-

[33]Alan H. Barton, *Studying the Effects of College Education: A Methodological Examination of Changing Values in College* (New Haven, Conn.: Hazen Foundation, 1959).

[34]Charles McClintock and Henry Turner, "The Impact of College upon Political Knowledge, Participation and Values," *Human Relations,* 15 (Fall 1962), 168–175.

[35]See David Riesman," The Jacob Report," *American Sociological Review,* 23 (December 1958), 732–738; Barton, *Studying the Effects of College Education,* pp. 31–35.

tion, the synthesis of cognitive and affective learning about political matters, has potential strength in the American culture. For instance, Middleton and Putney find that political expression is seldom a consequence of so-called adolescent rebellion. Only when parental interest in politics is substantial are students likely to channel their feelings toward unjust (overly permissive or overly punitive) parental discipline into politics.[36] For the majority of students without parental political concern to guide their energies, rebellion is likely to be manifest in a withdrawal from political concerns, a persistence of authoritarianism, and unwillingness to share tolerant viewpoints with their fellows. It is in this context that the expansion of political interests is potentially enriching to the burgeoning population of the vocational universities.

A related basis of support for vigorous political socialization is found in the generally bland nature of student political orientations. While college experiences appear to have little impact upon deep-seated political learning, such as political partisanship, it does seem to encourage the acquisition of broader perspectives about political events. Thus, the significant study by Dodge and Uyeki found that most students in a strongly Democratic environment retained their partisanship without the traumatic memory of crisis events, such as the Great Depression and the New Deal, that bolstered the Democratic partisanships of their parents.[37] This more flexible partisan commitment, in the context of a national political culture's eroding major cleavages among political groups, serves well the acquisition of more speculative and informed views about specific political matters.

There is a third sense in which the efforts of collegiate political socialization are potentially fruitful. Youthful activists, especially those in ideological rebellion, are most likely to rely on books and the mass media for political content. Most American college students who combine flexible partisanship with transient political interest rely on interpersonal experiences for their political opinions.[38] A rich mix of political socialization in the university can combine these intellectual and social bases of political learning

---

[36]Middleton and Putney, "Political Expression of Adolescent Rebellion," pp. 529–532.

[37]R. W. Dodge and E. S. Uyeki, "Political Affiliation and Imagery across Two Related Generations," pp. 220–223.

[38]See R. Middleton and S. Putney, "Influences on the Political Beliefs of American College Students," *Politico,* 29 (June 1964), 484–492.

in order to more broadly enhance the cognitive and social skills prerequisite to political participation. The college "egghead" and socialite can mutually draw on politics in the university in order to enrich their individual human development and that of the polity as well. The advantages of sociability for introverted or hostile political rebels is obvious. Less obvious is the critical evaluation of normal political socialization among college students. For instance, Far West residents, females, and political liberals were least likely to regard the probability of nuclear war involving America as likely in an important study.[39] However, the large majority of students interviewed thought that a nuclear war was probable and the mental acceptance of such a war was greatest among those with the most "sophisticated knowledge of international affairs" as measured by the authors. It would be interesting to know the sources of this information and their uncritical acceptance by the modestly informed majority. At the least, alternative sources of opinion, such as that held by political radicals and antiwar groups, would enhance the quality of public opinion on the campus.

However, this more generous view of political learning demands that a look beyond the range of socializing research reported here. It requires a politically critical orientation and more subtle indications of how personal values and education are made politically relevant. It is to such a prescriptive analysis of political learning that we now turn.

[39]S. Putney and R. Middleton, "Some Factors Associated with Student Acceptance or Rejection of War," *American Sociological Review,* 22 (October 1962), 655–667.

Chapter 8
Political Socialization: A Critical Appraisal

The effects of education on politics reviewed in Chapter 7 probably raise more questions than they serve to answer. One problem is that the concept of political socialization is basically concerned with the adaptation of citizens to the norms of the political system. Political socialization research has neglected issues of human development that enhance the ability of citizens to comprehend the political process. The central question in efforts to expand political education beyond mere vocationalism ought to ask how can college education effectively educate in order to maximize individual growth and political awareness?

The question of genuine political education has been raised in two ways within this chapter: first, by a critical evaluation of the political socialization concept; second, by an analysis of two case studies in which the values of the participants, which were influenced by the educational system, had direct political consequences. These two cases of political education were not merely instances where individuals were socialized into the existing system. Rather, these cases confront the question of appropriate learned behavior itself as a political issue.

THREE ELEMENTS IN POLITICAL SOCIALIZATION

As we have seen, the basic function of political socialization as it is presently conceived is to adjust individuals to the prevailing norms of the ongoing political system. However, as it has also been clearly illustrated, this narrowly defined function must be expanded and an alternative emphasis on the purpose of political education developed. There are three areas that must be considered before a broadened alternative to the present definition and function of political socialization can be achieved: the stability of the political system, the importance of self-concept as it is affected by the educational system, and the development of political concepts and value attainment.

An alternative emphasis on political socialization must include the impact of stability as an element of importance. The importance of attitudes toward the stability of the political system is most vividly seen in times of political crisis. One such case is the death of a system's political leader, in this case the assassination of John F. Kennedy, and its impact on the young. A major response to the assassination of President Kennedy by young American citizens was the affirmation of the American political system and Lyndon B. Johnson's succession to the presidency. If response to crisis provides the test of system stability, here was evidence of the social cement binding the American political order. Without this cohesion in the larger political system, a profound loss of political and personal orientation would have occurred.

Greenstein, summarizing the results of interviews among college students immediately after President Kennedy's death, describes the processes of denial, humor, and contact with loved ones designed both to reassure the individual of society's stability as well as to cope with the burdens of personal loss caused by the sudden death of a young and personable chief executive.

The death of the President was profoundly disturbing because it was a major fissure in the social order. Without this familiar figure in his regular position at the head of state, the security of the nation, both domestically and internationally, seemed problematic. Evidently, then, at least in our political system, the incumbent chief executive is a reassuring symbol of our social stability.[1]

Moreover, there is evidence which indicates that individuals least integrated into the American political system felt most upset about the assassination. For instance, in one study conducted after President Kennedy's death, 81 percent of all black children interviewed, but only 69 percent of all white children interviewed, reported that they "felt the loss of someone very close and dear."[2] Indeed, younger children (and children more than adults) wondered how the political system would endure in the absence of its major authority figure. Their responses were impulsively punitive in that two-thirds of the fourth-graders, but only 17 percent of the twelfth-graders, said that they "hoped the man who killed the President would be shot or beat up."[3]

These findings illustrate the importance of "anchorage" in the political order and the traumatic impact of disruption, especially upon those most vulnerable to the system's collapse. To propose a concept of political socialization that ignores the necessity of a functioning political system would be shortsighted. Yet concern with political stability, especially that of the American polity, has a way of feeding upon itself and producing a self-fulfilling prophecy, namely, that those most integrated within the system do (and should) learn participatory skills having potential political consequences.

The second element in a synoptic political learning perspective is the effect of educational systems upon the self-concepts of young citizens. There is now evidence that, as early as the fourth grade, school children can comment on a president's role perfor-

[1]Fred I. Greenstein, "College Student's Reactions to the Assassination," in Bradley S. Greenberg and Edwin B. Parker (eds.), *The Kennedy Assassination and the American Public: Social Communication in Crisis* (Stanford, Calif.: Stanford University Press, 1965), p. 239.

[2]Roberta S. Sigel, "Television and the Reaction of Schoolchildren to the Assassination," in Greenberg and Parker (eds.), *The Kennedy Assassination and the American Public,* pp. 199–219.

[3]Siegel, "Television and the Reaction of School Children to the Assassination," p. 217.

mance (not merely his personal qualities) in his handling of such issues as civil rights and the domestic economy. This latent political awareness can be significantly influenced by the school system.

For many children and young adults, the authority system of the schools themselves may constitute political socialization. Compliance in the face of authority may simply be a means of dealing with vulnerability in the face of superior power. It need not represent either the learning of political norms or the acquisition of knowledge to be applied in concrete situations having political meaning. Moreover, the combination of complaint responses and undue abstractions makes less meaningful the responses to such distant political objects as "the government" and "the American party system."[4]

The importance of relating self-concept to educational and political objects is evident in several studies. For instance, Litt's evidence indicates how difficult it is to teach participation and a view of politics as a dynamic process when the schools do not attempt to internalize these attitudes among urban school children.[5] Moreover, a narrow concept of political socialization obscures the evidence that the learning of school rules themselves may constitute pseudopolitics by reinforcing the authority patterns prevailing between students and teachers.[6] A view of political socialization that includes school efforts to maximize self-concepts is required if normal school processes are to support the attain-

[4] On the relationship among attitudes toward authority figures and children's political attitudes, see Fred I. Greenstein, *Children and Politics* (New Haven, Conn.: Yale University Press, 1965); Robert D. Hess *et al., The Development of Basic Attitudes and Values toward Government and Citizenship During the Elementary School Years,* Part I (Chicago: University of Chicago Press, 1965), pp. 380–385.

[5] See Edgar Litt, "Civic Education, Community Norms, and Political Indoctrination," *American Sociological Review,* 28 (February 1963), 73.

[6] Consider the situation that Hess *et al.* illustrate that teachers are more often perceived as having greater authority by low-status adolescents than by high-status adolescents, who have alternative sources of political information, including more open, participatory family experiences to draw on. In order to succeed in school, low-status adolescents are especially constrained to accept without criticism the teacher's unilateral determination of school rules. Thus, concludes the authors, conformity with school rules *becomes* the operational definition of "citizenship" for low-status adolescents.

ment of positive political attitudes. An interesting study of high school extracurricular activities and general effect (positive, neutral, or negative) toward American politics found a positive relationship among father's education level, frequency of participation in extracurricular activities, feelings of integration within the high school's status system, a general belief that people and institutions could be trusted, and a positive attitude toward American politics.[7] Indeed, those individuals who could probably most benefit from the political consequences of extracurricular participation and its resulting sense of enhanced social trust were least likely to participate in extracurricular activities.

The role of education as a supporting and compensatory system for enhancing self-concepts in political learning suggests that the school's authority system needs to support the lower-status child's self-concept in his relations with the school system. In essence, the school system itself, and its official relation to extracurricular activities, must provide the basis of social trust.

Third, a more generous concept of political learning includes the development of those external relationships in thought and action that put the young in touch with political realities. In addition to system stability and self-concept development, the broadening of conceptual boundaries is essential in political learning. There is evidence that in working-class or deprived homes sustained curiosity about relationships is not fostered or rewarded beyond immediate things and events to which the relationship refers. The resulting poverty of language and conceptual expression not only inhibits the development of abstract thinking needed to achieve in formal education, but also it serves to blunt the cultural and political consequences of education. As Suzanne Keller reports after observing two grade-school classes of American lower-class children:

> Participation and interaction with significant others in an organized way helps to shape the personality and sensitizes the participants to each other's needs and inclinations. Organized conversation helps shape the development of verbal

[7]David Ziblatt, "High School Extracurricular Activities and Political Socialization," *The Annals of the American Academy of Political and Social Science,* 361 (September 1965), 20–31.

facility and subtlety and determines a whole set of complex attitudes and feelings about the use of language.[8]

The element of value attainment in political learning also calls attention to the need for a synthesis of participation and cognitive attention to tools that will help the young citizen comprehend his environment. For instance, in a program at Northwestern University, Professor Anderson and his associates are teaching "distributive values" to urban students. The political implications of the program are grasped by one of the participants:

All of this [prescriptive political analysis] obviously involves social studies in controversial and politically explosive issues. We cannot, quite obviously, examine the supply and distribution of physical and mental health in American society without raising questions about the adequacy of justice or market mechanisms for the allocation of health resources. There is no way of avoiding controversy in social education without deliberately or inadvertently distorting the images of social life communicated to students.[9]

The consequences of attention to narrowly defined political socialization (namely, how effectively education increases general support of the political system) is only one criterion of political socialization. Political socialization also involves the transmission of experiences and concepts not normally found in urban school systems in order to enrich self-conceptualization and the perception of "real world" politics. Unwittingly, narrowly conceived political socialization has a conservative bias, for in stressing system stability it omits the more subtle development of personality and alternative definitions of political reality. The criteria of political

[8]Suzanne Keller, "The Social World of the Urban Slum Child: Some Early Findings," *American Journal of Orthopsychiatry*, 33:5 (1963), 823–831; see also Basil Bernstein, "Some Sociological Determinants of Perception: An Inquiry into Sub-Cultural Differences," *The British Journal of Sociology*, 1:2 (1958), 159–174.

[9]Lee F. Anderson, "Education and Political Science: Some Common Concerns," paper presented at a Conference on Education and Politics, Center for the Advanced Study of Educational Administration, University of Oregon, Eugene, Ore., June 14–17, 1966, p. 31.

learning are not given but are created in the application of enriched political learning. The absence of these other criteria reinforces "an antipolitical orientation [and] the failure to see politics as potentially, at least, an instrument of reason, legitimately dedicated to the improvement of social conditions."[10] It is to an intensive exploration of political consequences in educational situations and human values that we now turn.

NOW BRING TOGETHER: CASES IN VALUE ORIENTATION

A critique of socialization functional only within the purview of the existing political system and its vocational universities raises the responsibility to present some evidence about the consequences of other values in education. Two depth studies, one of school administrators and one of urban adolescents, sought to explicate consequences for political education.[11]

Consider first the behavior of twelve men who held key supervisory positions in the public school administration of a large Midwestern city. With but four exceptions, they had the following social characteristics:

Their fathers were professional men (most often ministers or educators) who lived in small towns or middlesized cities. After attending secondary school within the state, these schoolmen went East to a university and graduate school. After holding two or three school positions, they returned to their native state. Now in positions of considerable influence, they are socially integrated within the community. Residents of upper-status suburban communities, members of numerous social clubs catering to the plea-

[10]Christian Bay, "Politics and Pseudopolitics: A Critical Evaluation of Some Behavioral Literature," *American Political Science Review,* 59 (March 1965), 45. This is not an ideologist's call for an educational revolution; rather, it is awareness that more flexible concepts and action are required. In Marvick's realistic appraisal: "Learning about political life is not a simple, static, or finished process. Instead, it is highly complex; it is dynamic and changing, and, at best, it is imperfectly realized" (Dwaine Marvick, "The Political Socialization of the American Negro," *The Annals of the American Academy of Political and Social Science,* 361 [September 1965], 125).
[11]I am especially grateful for the cooperation of Mr. William Russell of the Milwaukee Boy's Club for his help in these studies.

sures of the professional-business strata, these schoolmen are in close contact with other elite groups within the community.

These men identify themselves with the "modern-liberal" wing of the education profession. Although most of them are Republicans, they favor vigorous federal action on behalf of school programs designed to bolster the quality of American education. Strong support of racial integration within the schools is at the core of their belief system. In general, an ethos of progressivism aptly applies to the schoolmen with these origins and values. However, their support of reform is checked by a high regard for the orderly processes of institutional life. Thus, they would turn the demands of direct action and overt protest into more traditional channels of communication.

Although values are propensities to "real world" behavior, they must be filtered through the realities of organized systems of behavior. Men's values are bound to conflict with their official, professional responsibilities. This kind of conflict was particularly acute in the confrontation of these twelve schoolmen with the demands of civic rights groups: The demands of the black community for more educational resources (skilled teachers, new integrated schools, advanced instruction) were consonant with the values of these liberal, nationally oriented schoolmen. However, when confronted with the consequences of these demands upon the operation of their own school system, these schoolmen resorted to a pattern of compensatory behavior in order to synthesize normative expectations and practical realities.

A normally placid Midwestern city was shaken by the panoply of techniques civil rights groups have used in order to demand better educational opportunities for black youth. For more than a year, boycotts, conferences with school officials, and "freedom schools" were used to change an existing informal system within the city's schools. That system was the pattern of assigning teachers, undertaking new school construction, and making policies within the school administration. As a result of long-standing customs that had hardened into political facts, four real, although completely unofficial, "districts" were used in making major school policies. Each district included a major section of the city characterized by distinct ethnic, social class, and residential patterns. The black community was included within the "inner district," and that district ranked low on a number of measures of educational quality, such as student-teacher ratio, median teacher qualifications and experience, and recent school construction and improvements. In fact, district priorities reflected effective demands among existing alliances of principles, parents, and community groups concerned about education. These demands guided the decisions of the school administration and the elected school board. Thus, decisions about teacher placement, budgetary allocations, and pupil transfers were made on the basis of these political precedents, precedents that did not benefit the black community in its quest for compensatory education.

The pressures of civil rights groups, however, did effect some changes. These changes were highly visible, but of limited scope, and were widely publicized in the metropolitan press and the internal house organs of the school system and its constituency. In summary, the intense activities of civil rights groups over a one-year period produced these results:

1. The proportion of the school budget allocated to the predominately black school district increased by only two percent.

2. There was no discernible change in the pattern of teacher mobility. The more experienced and better-qualified teachers remained concentrated in white residential areas, although many had begun their teaching in the city's inner core.

3. The pattern of new school construction was not changed. Major new constructions were planned in outlying areas of the city far removed from the predominately black district. Minimum renovation of existing structures and the rare purchase of another structure for conversion to educational use remained the pattern in the black district. Indeed, projections of educational needs, from playground space to the number of new teachers to be hired, were based on the existing allocation of resources; an allocation in which the black community fared poorly.

4. New changes in the curriculum, especially in the social studies program, were made rapidly. In response to civil rights demands, proposals for modernizing instruction, such as inclusion of material about anthropology and other behavioral sciences, were taken from indecisive school committees and approved by the schoolmen. As a result, the number of new courses in the black schools exceeded those introduced throughout the city.

5. There was a significant increase in the number of special programs designed to take care of academic needs among the culturally deprived. Concentrated in the predominantly black

schools, the programs were grafted onto existing school structure, so that newly hired professionals, many of whom were blacks, found themselves in much contact (and conflict) with older, locally oriented authorities in the school district. Proposals to directly link the special programs to the central school administration, thus bypassing the authority of indigenous principles and other local officials, were tabled. The inclusion of new content in the form of curriculum and special program reform was much easier to obtain than the administrative reorganization of authority patterns between the local school (and district) and the central school administration.

6. There was a sharp increase in the number of meetings and *ad hoc* committees formed to cope with the problem of quality, integrated education raised by the black community.

7. Contrary to more comprehensive but less visible reforms, a period of bussing small numbers of black students to predominantly white schools in outlying residential areas was initiated by the school administration. However, the program was terminated after it became a controversial issue among the city's lay school board. Although anticipating such a controversy, the schoolmen in this study found much symbolic value in token bussing as a means of showing goodwill toward the black community and of implementing their own values supporting integrated education.

It is important to consider those proposals that were not acted upon by the schoolmen in their official capacities within the school system. In every case, these suggestions, some of them quite radical in content, were accorded intensive consideration by the schoolmen. As is often the case, tolerance of new or controversial ideas is not the same as acceptance by individuals whose own system would be effected. After much consideration, proposals to reallocate existing and anticipated resources to black schools were tabled. For instance, available funds within the school budget could have been reallocated within the broad budgetary category of school construction. Such transfers were within the legal and administrative power of the central school officials and required no action by the school board or any other political body. In this way, some amenities to be refunded within new white schools could have been deleted and the funds applied to badly needed renovation of primary classroom and recreation facilities in the inner core.

Another proposal would have provided incentive pay for

qualified teachers to remain in the inner-core schools. Existing funds for teacher salary increments could have been used to reward teachers who remained in the inner-core schools. If adapted, the proposal might have reduced the flow of teacher skills away from the city's inner-core schools to schools with fewer "problems" (and greater conformity to the white, middle-class ethos) in residential sections. Once again, the approval of the school board or other public agencies was not needed to effect such changes. Indeed, it was precisely the administrative discretion available to make such innovations that appealed to thoughtful proponents of these measures. In neither case would other parties be seriously hurt by the shift in funds. The new schools to be constructed in white residential areas would be without such items as extra basketball courts, special acoustical materials, and spacious play areas. Teachers who did elect to transfer from inner-core schools to cosier residential areas would still receive pay increases and other benefits relative to their years of school service. The per capita reduction of these increments would be very small under the terms of the "core incentive" proposal.

It cannot be said that the schoolmen acted to bring about major structural changes within the community's schools. Their personal and professional socialization, their self-image as judicious managers of the "school plant," prevented any such view from becoming effective political action.

However, in the course of a heated political issue, the attitudes of the schoolmen toward integrated education remained unchanged. In the context of intense pressure from civil rights groups, consider alternative ways of resolving this conflict. First, the schoolmen could have reevaluated the special nature of black demands for quality education: At a most basic level, they could have attributed subtle, but pointed, hostile attributes to the black political leadership, evoked time-honored rationalizations about impatient radicals, and raised to a more abstract level those principles of educational equality to be sought in some distant time and under the aegis of other schoolmen.

A second alternative available to men of goodwill under political pressure is to consider the claims of the integrationists as one more item on the agenda of school politics. This pluralism of competing interests could justify limited expenditures of time and skill that the schoolmen devoted to the civil rights controversy. It could also rationalize a psychic withdrawal of the considerable personal stake these school professionals had in an integrated, high-quality public education. The intensity of that commitment vitiated this option in part because these men were liberal educators. Their self-image and professional socialization excluded the conscious realization that they were politicians to whom most positions were negotiable. Indeed, their disdain for professional politicians, especially those big-city politicians who catered to ethnic interests, increased their difficulty in relegating black school demands to the status of but another item on the educational agenda.

A third option was available to handle the gap between expectations and realities; namely, denial. In particular, these men could have denied that the school system they operated had failed to improve substantially the quality of education provided black youth. After all, they could point to the newly created committees, the special programs initiated with federal funds (but executed within the existing local school districts), and the major curriculum changes that revamped an archaic social studies program.

No doubt there were other options available to extract decision makers caught between their policy goal (sustained by personal commitment) and the realities of the educational system they administered (sustained in large measure by the professionalism of the same men). A combination of black demands seen in a less special framework requiring more routine consideration among competing school problems and a view that the school system was already satisfying these demands would have been particularly comforting to these schoolmen during the controversy.

Yet what emerged in response to the system behavior described was a strong pattern of positive personal behavior. It must be said that this behavior did not alter the incremental reform produced by the school system in response to sustained demands for much more by the black community. In this view, it can be argued that the personal values of the schoolmen were not only marginal to the performance of their official duties, but also subordinated to the requirements of system values. Thus, despite the personal socialization of our schoolmen as liberally educated sons of liberal parents, their allegiance to the school system required them to modify their official commitment to integrated, quality education. Karl Marx would have understood this process and so would students of organizational theory.

However, more sensitivity to the personal responses of the

schoolmen does sustain their allegiance to the values of integrated education. Although they did not challenge the basic organizational premises of the school system in which they held such prominent positions, the schoolmen were uncomfortably aware of the system's impediments to social change. Although they did not make sweeping changes in the school system, they did rescue badly needed curriculum revisions from the abyss of committee neglect. Thus, their official behavior in the face of black appeals for educational justice cannot be labeled as passive.

Indeed, the more these schoolmen were observed during the course of a politically critical year, the more clearly did their personal pattern of compensatory behavior in support of values form a pattern.

First, the schoolmen did not engage in any of the evasive patterns of thought and action enumerated above. At the end of a turbulent year, as at its beginning, they held firmly to the view that black youth had unique needs to be met by the city's schools. None of their attitudes or behavior can be said to have dishonored this claim.

Second, in accord with their initiative beyond their official roles, the schoolmen became very familiar with the dimensions of black education in the community. Anyone familiar with the working styles of "organization men" in this most organized society will appreciate that drastic changes in habit are uncommon. Consider also the allocation of time into segments to be used for scheduling appointments and conferences, the use of an agenda to structure the working day, the panoply of office buildings and conference rooms in which modern man spends his most alert waking hours. Now imagine a drastic change in these activities, especially the exploration of unfamiliar situations in which one's official role is exposed to critical evaluation. As the civil rights controversy grew in intensity and as the school system produced only the minimum changes noted, the schoolmen spent an increased amount of time examining the roots of the controversy. This included not only frequent visits to schools within the black community, but also extensive participation in discussions about the schools which were held within the homes of black parents and school children.

In addition, the schoolmen sought out educational innovations and demonstrations at the local university to better acquaint themselves with the latest developments available in coping with the problems of "de facto segregation." Nor can it be said that these experiences were transitory in nature. Indeed, the frequency and length of on-site investigations increased during the course of the year. The schoolmen's involvement in a very personal way grew almost in proportion to the limits of change they were able to effect in their official roles as school administrators. Nevertheless, the amount of personal participation described did have a profound effect on the attitudes of black community members throughout the year. The view of a school bureaucracy run by faceless administrators, essentially unconcerned with the welfare of black children, mellowed into feelings of deep, personal respect for the schoolmen who braved inclement weather to continually seek new understanding of the root problem.

It was through this pattern of compensatory personal behavior that the schoolmen were able to have some additional impact on the education of black children. As a result of their extra-official activity—often as a consequence of personal discussions with concerned parents—the schoolmen intervened in specific cases. For instance, requests for student transfers, allotment of special school equipment, or the hiring of special personnel to work in black schools were obtained through direct intervention of the school administrators. In marked degree, the schoolmen became socialized in a highly personal way to the concrete needs of the black school population. In fact, the more abstract "liberal" values of racially integrated education acquired richer meaning for the schoolmen, now experienced in many personal encounters with those for whom the quality of education was a daily problem.

The conflict between values and an existing pattern of socialization was also vividly present in the lives of black students. For almost a year the author and several associates conducted classes in civic education with twenty black, male adolescents. Weekly meetings were held on the premises of a social agency in the same Midwestern city in which incongruence between structures and values engaged our schoolmen. Most of these young men were members of the sponsoring organization; they came from stable families; and, with few exceptions, they were currently enrolled in one of the inner-district black high schools. Resentment about the quality of the schools and the uses of university research presented a problem. It was therefore necessary to create trust as well as rapport, and this meant providing instrumental values to the participants. We could have provided money or whatever status

gratification young black men would feel from the constant attention of white social scientists and their graduate students. Yet,
these considerations seemed trite and mechanical in the present
case. It may be a romantic illusion, but what still characterizes
social scientists is their professional knowledge about the operation
of political institutions.

It was this social exchange of knowledge for responses to our
questions that, in our opinion, propagated the climate of affection
in which our endeavors proceeded. Moreover, our information had
to be relevant to the felt needs of the participants. In the political
climate of the city in which our work progressed, as in so many
Northern cities, the relevant information was explicitly political.
Our exploration centered on the political processes of the city:
how key decisions were made, how to organize a precinct in an
election, the political party structure, and the connection between
voting and public policy formation. We discussed the structure and
operation of governmental agencies important to the lives of these
young men and their families. Information about welfare agencies,
the several extant programs charged with the elimination of poverty, and community pressure groups were examined.

Moreover, in each "lesson" we used concrete examples of
community action in social space familiar to our young participants. Here we used survey materials about their section of the
city and its relationship to broader political processes in the community. It was Karl Mannheim who argued that one should have
a say in the determination of one's life fate and that social
knowledge is necessary to improve the skills and knowledge ordinary men require for that task. In that spirit, our workshops
sought to relate the concrete personal needs of black adolescents
to the political processes of their community and, beyond that, to
the sketches of behavioral theories guiding our themes.

The thrust of the inquiry turned in time to the significance
of education. In hours of questioning, in probings designed to elicit
the structures of social thought elicited by the twenty young men
who, often at personal sacrifice, faithfully attended our Civics
Club, several themes reappeared relentlessly. Our inquiries about
the most visible community actors, such as the mayor and the city
council, yielded inconclusive responses. Divorced from either intense support or hostility, city hall and its inhabitants appeared
in the eyes of our respondents to be merely "there." They were
part of the political landscape unendowed with salient personal or

role qualities and disconnected from the life experiences and concerns of these young men.

The story was different when other authentic public figures, such as the police, were mentioned. Yet it was the educational system with its profound and intensely held problematic nature that most often held the attention of these young men. To be sure, our attention to these responses may reflect our own concern with political education, yet the frequency and intensity of collated responses suggests that we are reporting something other than selective perception.

The faith in education as the golden road to secular salvation and, with a more pragmatic eye, as the necessary prerequisite to any decent job and life is etched deeply on the consciousness of all these young men. "I mean without education you cannot get anywhere in life." It is John speaking, an intense, slender member of his high school's basketball team—and the others verbally assent to his forcefully spoken comments. Education, they all believe, is the key to personal fulfillment and will end the night of discrimination and poverty that plagues their parents and relatives.

The best evidence for the proposition that education is good for man and more education is valuable in solving society's ills, is found in the responses of a rare breed among our assembly: the high school dropout. Henry has been through the school system in a particularly revealing way. He began at North, a high school with a good academic reputation, and then was transferred to Central, a problem school in the city's core. His continuing and mounting disciplinary problems led him in a fatal way to the city's vocational high school.[12] After much effort, Henry managed to free himself of even this lowly scholastic status and to be dropped completely from man's effort to salvage his fellow man through grades and credits and the rationale of compulsory school attendance.

Yet—and this is the significance of Henry's contribution to our dialogue—his rebellion marks a deep personal concern for education. Not only does he assent to the general value of education, but also he can recall precisely the names of every teacher

---

[12]Incidentally, these boys are very perceptive about the status hierarchy within the city's high schools. As Henry commented: "I was so bad that they sent me to Vocational and that is really the end of the line." (The other boys nodded and verbalized agreement.)

and the subject matter of each course in his Odyssey of travail through the city's high schools. No mark of apathy or rebellion can cloud Henry's abiding faith in education. While complaining about the white, middle-class expectations of some teachers (but not all), he knows what he has lost and weighs his fate accordingly. As one may say, in traditional Catholic theology, that the Church temporal errs while the Church eternal remains omnipotent, so, in the mind of this dusky young citizen, does the sanctity of education remain despite the behavior of its all too human representatives.

The mystique of the curriculum also looms large in these discussions. We had expected in the course of our discourses to find the problems of the schools in interpersonal relations, in the conflict between black and white, in the disputations between the expectations of adults and the probings of youthful behavior. Yet, while uncovering traces of these tensions with others and authority, there is a more subtle persistent process at work in these proceedings. I ask Bob about a particular history course we have been discussing, a subject made relevant by our previous investigation of the city's budding programs in the welfare fields and the origins of newly created efforts to eradicate poverty. Bob is normally articulate and responsive, but here he is fumbling for an answer. "I don't know—the history they teach us is about olden times. It seems that I don't find myself a party to it." There is no mention of Martin Luther King and the civil rights movement or the insights to be gained by comparing the Athens of Socrates with the Black Belt of contemporary freedom fighters.

What occurs here and what reappears so often in the remarks of the other boys is a bewilderment not about school routine or teacher authority, but about the rationality of their subject matter (especially in the humanities and social studies). Now it may be said with some truth that these are the observations of semiliterate, semieducated black urban youth. After all, minority status and powerlessness are not eternal virtues that, in the nature of things, point up the inadequacies of the existing "system." Yet this interpretation misses the point, because in discussions ranging from community politics to the social structure of American society these young men have shown capacities, previously untapped, to grapple with the implications of social thought. In the realm of experience encountered with formal education, Bob is plainly puzzled: "I don't know—the truth is that I have no notion of what I am supposed to take away with my schooling, what it is saying to me as a black and as a man."

It is precisely here in the absence of *verstehen* about processes so patently critical to one's life fate that behavior patterns acquire a larger significance. Like their ancestors rooted in the "natural order" of the plantation system, no one (except in the crisis atmosphere of a "freedom school") has explained the rationality of their school program. In this state of affairs, the vitality of these expressive young men is treated as antisocial behavior and a threat to educational processes. To defer impulses for a known, if distant, goal is one thing; to act as if the curriculum spoke to them is, in their eyes, a self-denying act, and since they are not ashamed of their bodies and feelings, a calculated response is forthcoming.

It is in this context, I believe, that the responses to authority by these socially integrated young men can be understood. Deprived of a comprehensive explanation for their own program of studies and its meaning to their own behavior, the petty testing of principal and teacher authority in adolescent experiences assumes larger proportions. A natural openness to exploration evident in our discourses is stunted on behalf of interests threatened by the incongruity between the curriculum and the young men's personal style. The problem is that the meaning and rationale of "civilization," insofar as it appears in the authoritative school system, is mute in the mouths of those who carry the teacher college's burden to the city's inner core.

What follows is a partial withdrawal from the experiences and problems of urban man that could enliven him. It seems that these young men are asking to be included, not in the formal sense of curriculum making, but in the ego sense of having their feelings and movements included within the learning processes. The rigid ordering of seats, the endless bells and rules that make more vivid the marginal differentiation between the roles and life styles of teacher and student, avoiding the subject matter, styles of dress and speech, and their threat to the teacher's status, are constantly in the foreground of controversy and discussion. The accompanying motive for these acts lies less in race problems or, in the case of these young men, in the rejection of education than in the protection of self-esteem.

This protection of self-esteem that occupies so much efficacy of students and school behavior makes "thou shalt not cut on me" an apt motto of urban education's dynamics. In light of the non-rational perception of school processes and teacher-student relations, its urgency is heightened in classroom and school assembly. "I wish he would stop cutting on me so," responds Frank when asked about his relations with his major teacher. "I walk into the room [attired in pegged pants] and right away he says 'Look, the troublemaker is here again.' Man, I don't want no trouble so I wish he wouldn't get on me for everything." Beyond social difficulties and the temperaments of generations, the absence of a meeting ground in subject matter and its relation to self enhances the "cutting up" view of teacher roles that these young men hold. In this context, there is little rational behavior left except to protect self-esteem with the varied (and often disturbing) means of the young. Feeling themselves rejected in the educational processes, school becomes the forum for acting out these problems between students and teachers.

Except for Henry, who has given up and dropped out of the system, the behavior of these young men is more prudential, a more self-rewarding response to education's ambiguities as expressed in the urban core school. Valuing education as an ideal endowed with almost magical qualities, the symbiotic patterns of teacher-student relations lacking personal trust and meaning are often destructive. Yet these young men are not fools; they are aware of education's influence on their lives. Thus, they cut up at the margins, testing the teacher's authority boundaries while carefully refraining from going too far and being dropped from the only system able to provide them the credentials to the adult world of work and status. This prudential strategy of "cutting up at the margins" testifies not only to their reality-bound orientation; it also argues against an alternative view, namely that these young men cannot defer gratifications or their impulses. On the contrary, the cutting up at the margins is an effective device for protecting their self-esteem *and* adapting realistically to adult requirements. The rewards of this behavior permit the young men to graduate, while protesting that the graduation has not included subject beauty or system affinity to their personal life situations.

Yet, in drawing a balance sheet, the costs involved should not be ignored. First, much time, energy, and emotional feeling go into the marginal disputations between the formal educational system and its young charges. There is a kind of petty industrial sabotage at work in these processes. It is not an effort comparable to achieving worker control over management or even an effort to secure higher wages. Rather, it is an effort to be included within the system so that the rationale of the operations involves, in a human sense, the needs and life styles of those involved.

Second, the costs of the prudential marginality described include those values of insight and sensibility that have always been the fruits of a liberating education. Despite the disadvantages of their racial plight, the young men described herein do survive the school system and will become partially functioning members of the adult world. But they do not know—no one has taught them to know—what can possibly be involved in the term "liberal education." And this loss must be weighed against the brave efforts of an educational system to prepare all for life.

Chapter 9
Politics
and the University:
A Summary

POLITICAL CONSEQUENCES OF VOCATIONALISM

Educational systems have always been influenced by the dominant drift of the society of which they are a part. In an era when regional politics and social life prevailed, a mosaic of private and denominational colleges independently advanced the interests of their founding sects. When the national political culture and industrial framework was being constructed, the state universities rose to positions of influence in American life. Today, higher education is intimately linked with every major social institution, from the research-minded corporation to the social welfare programs of the federal government. This transformation, developed at an accelerating tempo in the last two decades, has made the relationship between knowledge and power complete. The pursuit of national power and specialized expertise has led to the transformation of major universities from centers of education to bastions of research and training designed to propel the existing order. In the process, established institutions have adapted themselves to the requirements of national eminence and power. Furthermore, a pure type of knowledge service organization, the large vocation-oriented university, has developed in harmony with these new conditions. While earlier knowledge centers had a cultural base in the ethos of a social class, the tenants of scientific rationalism, or the development of applied knowledge, the vocational university was born without any independent heritage. As the product of the national political economy, it represents the fusion of knowledge to power, of applied to basic learning, of social requirements to the main drift of the welfare state.

It is in this context that once more the question of education as personal cultivation and human development is raised, because nothing in the experience of the vocational university and the skilled technocrats who run it suggests the relevance of this inquiry. All criticisms of major social institutions involve a selection from the diversity of empirical reality. Robert Hutchins has criticized the universities for being too vulgar, too acquisitive in a manner unsuited for sacred temples of learning which ought to be devoted to long-term contemplation. Veblan thought that the anti-intellectualism of the university in his day and its business managers attuned to the cash nexus were malevolent forces. There is, in addition, a long tradition of populist and utopian criticism, most recently expressed in student protest movements, that bemoans the scale and impersonality of contemporary knowledge centers. Yet this romance of communitarianism fails to confront the problems of scale, which makes college opportunities available to almost every social strata, and complicates the political economy. In all of these critiques, there is a fundamental strain, a search for an intellectual paradise amidst the shadings of the present order.

An analysis of the vocational university ought to be more attuned to these shadings and social consequences. First, in its provision for broad opportunity, the public vocational university articulates in modern idiom a base value of equalitarianism, a value that has particular meaning to racial minorities and lower-status youth in a modern society. Second, the pursuit of vocationalism itself is a realistic response to the job expectations and economic directions of our affluent society. Third, in its pragmatic application of universal norms and contractual relations, the public vocational university dilutes the ideological base of alienated intellectuals whose past perspectives have contained more than a modicum of projected sentiment about the social order. Fourth, in the process of civic socialization, the vocational university is functional in that it reinforces commitments and skills that support the political system.

On the other hand, the socially functional university becomes the focal point of critical stresses in the correlation between knowledge and power and in the life styles of its graduates. In a personal sense, a university education has provided the opportunity for a transition from the world of the child and the adolescent to that of the knowledgeable adult. Psychologists are more likely to think of identity diffusion, sociologists of role experimentation, humanists of cultural acquisition in the drama of the human condition, and students of politics to emphasize political learning in terms of participatory styles and skills useful to the citizen should he choose to develop a lasting interest in public affairs. The essential point is that personal and social development intertwine; the knowledgeable member of a political public has some criteria with which to evaluate events.

The contradictions within the vocational university from this perspective are considerable. A technically functional institution, the vocational university promotes an ahistorical view of political and social life although it is, in fact, the historically specific product of a society at the height of its power and scientific sophistication. Although its rapid expansion has been predicated on the vastly expanded demand for a college education among the lower-middle and working classes, the vocational university constricts the flow of this demand into the functionally specific channels of a social escalator. The product of immense cultivation of personal and organizational resources, it does not promote the growth of personal sensibility or the imaginative use of organizational forms to enrich the curriculum and the student culture. An outgrowth of political and economic dynamism, it creates an authority system and internal structure promoting passivity among those students most in need of active and self-esteeming experiences. Although based on the growth of scientific knowledge that at its best challenges conventional wisdom, it blends into the educational landscape and reduces to false equality the myriad of activities pursued within its benign framework. At a time when interest in personal cultivation and political perspectives are greatest among young adults, it takes refuge in an institutional objectivity substantially different from the suspension of belief that marks the creative scientific enterprise.

There is, to be sure, a case to be made that the vocational university produces incremental gains for society and individuals, that it equalizes its graduates and reduces the incidence of anomie and social distrust. There is another case to be made that precedes from the supposedly value-free nature of the vocational university, its formal and informal organization, and its openended relationship with sources of governmental and corporate power. That case is based on the explicitly political function of the vocational university. That function is to expand the scope of rationalized knowledge and apply it to the solution of concrete social problems. The collective enterprise devotes itself to these tasks, while the "educational" function is to train more individuals with applied skills. The relationship between personal training of future role-incumbents and the collective function is mutually supporting.

Yet, a set of institutions with "built-in" definitions of history and mission is not politically neutral. The consequence on the personal and collective level is to discard alternative perspectives by which men can understand political life and their potential role within it. The vocational university is not hospitable to the broad range of humanities and intellectual speculation or to the explication of value questions that can fruitfully engage the intellectual resources of the young. Moreover, there is a tendency to regard criticism as pathological or dysfunctional and, beyond that, to constrict attention to the impact of political and social events on the educational process itself. These consequences are due in small measure to the malevolence of individual actors or the denial of academic freedom and student rights. Rather, the tendency is for the academic and social agenda to be given in a technoscientific natural order, whose functions are efficiently performed by the public vocational universities. In structure and process, the public vocational universities have been created to provide answers to questions that have already been preselected. Those questions revolve about the utility of applied research for corporate and governmental agencies at the collective level and about the internalization of specific task-related skills for the individual. It is the cultivation of intellectual sensitivity, participatory skills, and political awareness that are most easily and almost imperceptibly sacrificed in the long run.

EDUCATION AND POLITICS

The consequences of the public vocational university are closely related to the relationship between education and political learning. In numerous studies, higher education has been positively correlated with greater tolerance, participation, and civic allegiance. Yet the processes within the educational experience themselves are less confidently assessed. The paradox of the public vocational university is that its potential consequences for the political orientations of its lower-middle and working-class students exceeds that of elite colleges, where the student is less likely to be radically changed by his education. From the point of human development, the mass-based university can particularly deal with the cynicism and lack of political criticism that are the products of family and peer learning among its student body. Here too the university is a potential force in counteracting the pervasiveness of mass youth culture.

In part, the civic condition in the public vocational university is due to its size and structure; in part, too, it represents a considered hierarchy in which the questions raised are less highly valued. Moreover, the internal structure of the public vocational university in the developmental consequences of its curriculum, faculty instruction, and student culture are not geared to basic social and intellectual inquiry. However, the generic problem concerns the impact of articulated values on the life styles of the student. Some attempt to make this relationship explicit guided the case studies analyzed in Chapter 8. A more comprehensive effort to understand the interaction of knowledge and power through the conduit of the welfare state university becomes, in this perspective, the central task of its undergraduate education.

In other educational systems, knowledge and the individual's personal and public relation to it were officially communicated in the pronouncements of priests, ministers of education, professors, and other authorities. At times too the cohesive value system of a region, ethnic group, or social class provided the basis for detached inquiry. None of these conditions is present in the current situation, so that the subject of value orientation and empirical evidence of its transmission becomes a collective inquiry among professionals and students. Thus, the root question of the public vocational university is not its authority structure, its shaping of the student culture, or its functional specificity for socializing the young to the tasks and prevailing politics in the society. The root question becomes the criteria of intellectual choice themselves and the manner by which the rapport between institutional power systems shapes choice. The proper study of the public vocational university from the perspective of human development and political sensitivity is the vocational university itself as a socializing agency of expanding influence.

The "College of General Studies"[1] has, at various times, concerned itself with the liberal arts designed to produce cultivated young men and young women, the ascendency of scientific knowledge in a complex society, and the more diffuse set of courses representing the accumulation of scholarly interests and social demands. Each development provided its own perspective supplemented at times by a rich student culture linking academic and social concerns. Only extreme ethnocentrism would support a contemporary view in which the university, especially its welfare-oriented offsprings, provided such an outlook to guide cognitive and affective learning. Original inquiry is the province of an unprecedented range of research centers and institutes. Explicit examination of public policy and administration increasing falls within the purview of specialized governmental agencies, which train their personnel in current knowledge. Professional specialities, from medicine to counterintelligence, develop their specific criteria of selection and range of essential knowledge. In this context, general studies focusing upon the social and political implications of the public vocational university provide a common orientation for the burgeoning student populations in future decades.

A reconstructed perspective on a mass society's college education begins with the pragmatic instructional and research links of the public vocational university to a polity dominated by specialized expertise and professional knowledge. The dual functions of enhancing job skills and socializing individuals to the ongoing political system are propelled by strong forces in the economy and the polity. While these functions cannot be ignored or radically changed, it is nevertheless possible to enhance a cultural base in education that is oriented toward the articulation of human needs and the fruition of critical learning. This supportive base can be fashioned within the curriculum and student culture of the voca-

---

[1]"College of General Studies" is a collective term referring to all liberal arts colleges or other universities providing a general as opposed to a vocational education.

tional university. The external supports include the use of elite youth culture, social organizations, and intellectual perspectives on major public policies and their consequences within the vocational university itself.

In a curious way, a number of developments have potentially freed the large university to make humane and civic education relevant to the contemporary needs of its students. One of these developments is the vast expansion of opportunities for higher education, opportunities that have mitigated the class basis of the higher learning. In an earlier period, the university imparted the ethos and values of middle-class life. Moreover, the formal educational system held a near monopoly on the nature and evaluation of social knowledge. Today, the cultural role of the universities has been muted and other major social institutions compete with the university in the opinion market. In addition, the specialization of research and policy-forming activities has impinged on the dominance of the university as a source of social action. Relieved of these former obligations, the contemporary university, especially its undergraduate education, is uniquely suited to provide broad-gauged induction to the contemporary interrelation between knowledge and power. As an appendage of the knowledgeable society, the vocational thrust can be augmented by considerations of how social institutions influence human development.

PERSONAL INTEGRATION
AND POLITICAL DEVELOPMENT

A combination of speculative and empirical study of the university as an instrument of political power and social knowledge raises anew the classic questions of substance that have attracted the interests of inquisitive youth. The failure to articulate these concerns and to integrate them within the vocational university's structure increases the appeal of the mass youth culture with its unreflective perceptions of contemporary life. Such mass influences produce a sporadic and segmented orientation to substantive policy issues that have human consequences below the abstract level of system maintenance. In this context, the personal guidance of sages and parents becomes institutionalized in a viable learning environment devoted to a synthesis of social knowledge. On the personal level, contemporary civic education provides available resources with which the student may participate in his education and social development. On an institutional level, reinforcing supports within curriculum and student culture emphasize connections between formal and informal interaction about the university's mission in contemporary society. In a larger sense, the examination of major social issues, such as poverty, war, and human rights, places the developmental role of the university in a meaningful context.

The cumulative impact of formal education remains a matter of open inquiry. Extant evidence that education has a liberating effect is largely based on examinations of quality colleges and universities with substantial intellectual content. Furthermore, there is conflicting evidence about the link between student culture and formal educational processes. The potential framework for political learning in the vocational university does not include strong countervailing forces rooted in the culture of a social class or substantive political concerns. Its greatest impact is on narrow cognitive skills associated with the performance of specific tasks in complex organizations. It leaves unchanged the affective and evaluative elements of learning that are only partly formed by prior family and peer influences. The end product may well be technical expertise without the breadth of social and personal development required for autonomous consideration of genuine political choice.

In a profound sense, the vocational university connotes the supreme rationalization of intellect in the form of applied learning. The advantages here are in learning the instrumental norms of society and the importance of them to the stability of the political system. The disadvantages accrue from this one-dimensional perspective in which questions of perception, judgment, and policy consequences are slighted. A knowledge-based society requires technical competence to prosper, but it also needs criteria of prudential judgment to guide personal and political behavior. Formal rationality is but one short step from social rationalization in which the human dimension of foreign policy and governmental decisions is absent. The formal rationality within the vocational university and its cool relations with its students erodes political education once located in the social studies and the faculty. The richness of the cultural base within the vocational university and the consequences of subsequent learning for its students provide a useful test to judge the civic quality of global decisions made by a nation at the height of its power. In the critical experiential base of the modern society's university will be planted the seeds of civic capacity and reflection that will influence the human quality of the polity in coming decades.

The political thrust of university education has been three-fold; namely, to promote allegiance to the political system, to provide interpersonal experiences enhancing participatory skills, and to liberalize attitudes about civil liberties and democratic norms. Although the empirical sequences among these outcomes and the educational process are uncertain, formal education has been thought to be a significant agency of these political orientations. The context of the vocational university does not encourage the continuous transmission of these values in the future. Nor, in a prescriptive concern with human need fulfillment, is there reason to assume the inevitable perpetuation of these outcomes. Thus, in one sense the public vocational university is more divorced from political learning than the urban high school, the elite college, or the state university in a period of educational and intellectual underdevelopment. On the other hand, the public vocational university is a creature of the welfare state and, thus, more intimately related to governmental agencies and public knowledge than any university system in American history. The dissonance between the institutional and personal realities of the vocational university provides the framework for the analysis offered in this book. A product of the end of ideology in a period of unprecedented rapport between educational and political systems, the vocational university is a superb offspring of formal rationality in contemporary learning. Its future impact on the substantive rationality, personal development, and political orientation of its graduates remains an open question for the political sagacity of a knowledgeable society.

POLITICAL OBLIGATION AND DISSENT IN THE KNOWLEDGEABLE SOCIETY

Yet the openended nature of university and government relations does not mean that the acceleration of certain trends is beyond our insight. First, it is clear that the content and symbols of social knowledge are critical to the formulation and execution of major public policies. Although individual intellectuals may become ornaments to men of power, the systematic products of the American knowledge system are now indispensable to policy justifications in national defense, race relations, and foreign policies. It is no longer wise to argue political viewpoints on the basis of personal charisma or ideological passion. The maturation of system analysis, political opinion polling, and mass communication analysis means that social knowledge is a critical element in every political decision. Concomitantly, the scope of the American knowledge system requires politicians to speak in those terms desired by the increasingly educated sectors of the society. The language of physical and behavioral sciences becomes to modern politics what popular rhetoric or knowledge of the common law were in earlier periods. Under these conditions, the uses and styles of public knowledge become dramatically altered. It becomes necessary for all political agencies to locate an intellectual rationale and train personnel who pass muster under these conditions. The consequences for American foreign policy are very interesting, given the articulation of the political intellectual style:

> As in the US, the CIA in Vietnam prides itself on being more catholic than overt governmental agencies . . . the CIA has a real affinity with ex-leftists and pseudo-leftists of all stripes, as well as with the radical right. It likes intellectuals, which is natural, first because they are walking repositories of information, and second because the CIA sees itself as a lonely master-mind, the poet and unacknowledged legislator of the government. Finally the CIA, collectively speaking, is an auto-didact which never had time to get its Ph.D. and yearns to meet real, motivated political theorists and oddballs and have a structured conversation with them. The relentless resort to academic jargon about the war in Vietnam, on the part of half-educated spokesmen and commentators, doubtless reveals the CIA influences on people who may be unaware of it.[2]

Moreover, the use of social knowledge as a base for political power also requires new political techniques. It is much more effective to control the sources and products of the society's knowledge base than it is to silence intellectuals or to engage in irrational

[2]Christian Bay, "Beyond Pluralism: The Problem of Evaluating Political Institutions in Terms of Human Needs," Conference on Social Scientists and the Normative Analysis of Political Life (Evanston, Illinois, May 1966 [mimeo]), p. 23.

public oratory. In a society that values expertise, the criteria of expertise itself become politically critical. Thus, the major political conflicts are about specific policies in the context of relevant social knowledge. Although there is opinion to the contrary, we are witnessing the modern, "rational," version of ideology in action. The dissociation of knowledge from its prior social meanings is a major factor in policy formation:

> It is peculiar that the academic experts who have been studying guerrilla techniques, Communism, "wars of liberation," for nearly two decades have been unable to face the question of intention in this kind of warfare, where combatants and noncombatants are all but inseparable, while the means of killing and exterminating have been reaching a point close to perfection. For knowledge of the consequences of an action that is then performed generally argues the will to do it: if this occurs repeatedly, and the doer continues to protest that he did not will the consequences, this suggests an extreme and dangerous dissociation of the personality.[3]

In more historical depth, the influence of theologians, humanists, and legalists has declined, and their sacred texts are disregarded by current policy experts. The liberal competition of political ideas in the public marketplace is transformed into competing systems of knowledge markets themselves. Herein, the most effective way to develop political power and to silence one's critics is to ignore the questions raised on the grounds that they stem from a knowledge base that is socially irrelevant. The expansion and high tempo of public knowledge institutions creates applied, or "technoknowledge," that accelerates the automation of old social knowledge bases and their political concerns. This process is not neutral, because it is itself influenced by the needs of major corporate and political institutions, with the public vocational university's providing efficiency criteria for producing the knowledge product. Nor is technoknowledge the only manifestation of the conjunction of power and knowledge as they have evolved in the expansive domain of our society.

For instance, in the controversy about university draft ex-

[3]Mary McCarthy, "Vietnam III: Intellectuals," *The New York Review of Books* (May 18, 1967), 7.

emptions, it is significant that the biological and physical sciences are most highly valued. Evidently there is a collective judgment that animals and anthropologists are less important to the national needs of the public knowledge system. Moreover, the struggle about knowledge bases and the policies needed to justify them increasingly resembles industrial policies of a modernizing society. Herein, the humanists and theologians find themselves in contracting industries; that is to say, in the same position as textiles and coal after the nation had satiated its need for raw power. The national Institute for Humanities, a recently created federal research-supporting agency, serves as a protective tariff agency for intellect analogous to that extracted by New England manufacturers and Appalachian coal operators when their products were threatened by more modern, efficient, and cheaper products. The political issue about what is reliable knowledge also influences the collective judgment of university systems in their allocation of scarce resources.

Moreover, advances in the public knowledge system raise the issue of mutual obligation between those who support and those who execute these processes. It is not clear that the private patron of artistic or political knowledge exerted more control in his era of domination than is presently exerted by the federal government on the universities. The point is that cumulative socialization within the modern knowledge system does produce a sense of obligation to the contract-granting state. The American knowledge revolution has progressed from static collegiate and private relations to a network of federal contractual relations. The rewards so eagerly sought and obtained might produce a sense of contractual fealty analogous to the nobility's sense of felt obligation to the medieval monarch. This is not to suggest that scholars and intellectual technicians are timid personalities. Rather, it is the logical culmination of a reward system in which precise public knowledge is most highly valued.

Herein is created a strong sense of allegiance to the American political system and a tendency to avoid delicate questions about national power and policy. The national public vocational university is the epitome of organized knowledge exploiting supposedly technical, apolitical, and ahistorical data. The assimilation of research professionals strengthens the contemporary political contract between the members of the knowledge industry and their counterparts in government and corporate offices. It is no longer possible for professional and scholarly associations to avoid political alliances with respect to contractual and individual research. Studies of war and peace, applied behavioral science, and urban problems have revealed a deep penetration of the federal government and national corporate structure into established centers of public knowledge. Redirected to cope with public and social problems defined by officialdom, the citizens of the public vocational university are increasingly government-made men, and they have learned well the dictates of contractual prudence.

No more vivid case of this new contractual obligation is evident than in the impact of American involvement in Vietnam upon the vocational university. Despite the visible criticism among some scholars and universities, the typical response in the vocational university has been one of institutional avoidance. There has been little institutional statement on controversial public issues, and in the typical case only a small minority of academics and researchers have expressed their views. The critical link here is between the maturation of a national vocational university system and the compartmentalization of specialized professional university. Thus, even within the discipline of political science (a subject supposedly relevant to major policy issues), the stance of scientific neutralism has developed with respect to the uses of knowledge by public agencies.

It was the genius of Bismarck to combine a nation's need for mass education with fundamental loyalty to the expanding German political culture of his day. By enhancing the status and privileges of German academicians and teachers within the universities, Bismarck was able to extract an implicit agreement that no major social criticism would be directed against his policies for nationalizing Germany. In contemporary America, the institutional base of the typical public vocational university is vulnerable to political pressures. Lacking independent fiscal and intellectual resources, the institutional managers of vocationalism are wary about political uses of resources lest there be a depression on the grant and subsidy markets. Erich Hoffer, among other social analysts, has long maintained that intellectuals aspire to be courted by men of power. The consequence of this desire for the critical faculties of a knowledge industry that is dependent upon governmental largess remains a thorny problem of political obligation.

The question of political obligation is complemented by a major issue of social control. Universities have often been used to propound an accepted political creed, becoming a system of indoctrination designed to protect the young against heretical ideas. Control over the public uses of knowledge is enhanced by limiting access to the instruments of knowledge to a small and trusted coterie. However, a small knowledgeable elite is impractical within a society motored by the products and processes of basic and applied research. Thus, the systematic development and rationalization of the American knowledge system has not been without conflict. Internally, status and class divisions have developed within the major universities and between teaching and research staffs. Yet more serious than these highly publicized phenomena has been the countercyclical use of the university as a site of political criticism and action. From the civil rights core of the Berkeley Free Speech movement to public criticism about Vietnam within parts of the academy, the development of the American knowledge system has also increased the expertise and resources of those who use social knowledge in politically critical ways. While requiring the collective products of the knowledge system, political leaders are concerned about the personal and social uses of knowledge to openly debunk their policies. Indeed, the initiation of antiwar criticism of America's Vietnam policy was largely a matter of selective uses of university resources.[4] Seldom have individuals connected with higher education been so responsible for propogating a national discussion of American policy.

By contrast, the purely vocational university is more amenable to social control because it is more dependent upon public directions and support for its varied activities. Thus, it is probable that the critical intellectual will become a relic of a past age, one to be replaced by the "professional" knowledge worker whose public opinions are compartmentalized from his intellectual and occupational endeavors. It is such a completely impersonal and rationalized system that has always animated a particular scientific genre of behavioral research. It thrives on a control of human behavior that is insensitive to human need and the political measures required to sustain it.

Only the balanced effort to synthesize cognitive and affective knowledge, of objective and public scholarship, and of skill and

[4]Christian Bay, "The Cheerful Science of Dismal Politics," in *The Dissenting Academy,* edited by Theodore Roszak (New York: Pantheon Press, 1968), pp. 208–230.

cultivated learning will sustain the polity that currently implants the vocational impulse in most educational undertakings. The modern American knowledge system has provided unprecedented social and economic support to the political economy. It has also been more than willing to work closely with the political and military establishments to bring about such uses of knowledge as these:

> A new type of officer appeared in the field with a traveling library; on the bookshelves in his mountain hideout were the works of Mao, General Giap, and Ho Chi Minh. Young West Pointers were turned into political strategists on the spot by the crash course in Communism and native psychology. . . . The same year—1961—that the Special Forces was created, the Staley Plan was devised by a Stanford economist, Eugene Staley, whose name is now identified with Strategic Hamlets, though his plan, in fact, was much more comprehensive and undertook a complete restyling of the Vietnamese economy, the political struggle and the AID program.[5]

Therefore, it is imperative that the burgeoning American knowledge system receive a new combination of mass resources and humane cultivation in order that it remain capable of providing allegiant criticism to government and private group policies that threaten to destroy the meaning of social knowledge, while expanding its voracious technical outreach. Herein, self-consciousness is the first step in developing an academic political culture suitable to the needs of the most highly educated and most violent period in the knowledgeable society's history.

[5]McCarthy, p. 13.

Index